Basic Bible Sermons on Psalms
for Everyday Living

BASIC BIBLE SERMONS

ON
PSALMS FOR EVERYDAY LIVING

James T. Draper, Jr.

BROADMAN PRESS
NASHVILLE, TENNESSEE

© Copyright 1992 • Broadman Press
All rights reserved
4222-80
ISBN: 0-8054-2280-3
Dewey Decimal Classification: 223.2
Subject Heading: BIBLE. O.T. PSALMS - SERMONS
Library of Congress Catalog Card Number: 92-2616
Printed in the United States of America

Scripture quotations are from the
King James Version of the Bible.

Library of Congress Cataloging-in-Publication Data

Draper, James T.
   Basic Bible sermons on Psalms for everyday living / James T.
Draper, Jr.
      p.   cm. — (Basic Bible Sermons Series)
   ISBN 0-8054-2280-3 :
   1. Bible. O.T. Psalms—Sermons. 2. Sermons, American.
3. Southern Baptist Convention—Sermons. 4. Baptists—Sermons.
I. Title. II. Series.
BS1430.4.D73   1992
252'.061—dc20

                                                        92-2616
                                                        CIP

To William E. Bell, Jr.
With great appreciation and love
for your
counsel, guidance, friendship, and encouragement
over many years

Other Books in the Basic Bible Sermons Series:
Basic Bible Sermons on the Cross, W. A. Criswell
Basic Bible Sermons on Hope, David Albert Farmer
Basic Bible Sermons on Philippians, J. B. Fowler
Basic Bible Sermons on John, Herschel H. Hobbs
Basic Bible Sermons on Easter, Chevis F. Horne
Basic Bible Sermons on Christmas, Chevis F. Horne
Basic Bible Sermons on Spiritual Living, Stephen B. McSwain
Basic Bible Sermons on Handling Conflict, Paul W. Powell
Basic Bible Sermons on Christian Stewardship, J. Alfred Smith, Sr.
with J. Alfred Smith, Jr.
Basic Bible Sermons on the Church, Ralph Smith
Basic Bible Sermons on the Ten Commandments, Jerry Vines

Contents

1
The Truly Happy Person

Psalm 1

Numerous scholars of the Old Testament believe Psalm 1 is the epitome of all the psalms. These six stanzas set the tone for all 150 psalms and present an overview and introduction to the psalms and to the psalmist.

For instance, this initial psalm states there are only two kinds of people—godly and ungodly, wise and foolish. This truth is a given. You are either with God or against Him. This calls to mind the observation of Jesus: "He that is not with me is against me; and he that gathereth not with me scattereth abroad" (Matt. 12:30). That contrast and delineation continues throughout the entire book.

The Book of Psalms is a portion of what is called Wisdom Literature. Wisdom Literature contains practical counsel God has given to help us in our everyday lives. Throughout Psalms there is the contrast between the wise man and the foolish. The opposite of wisdom is not ignorance. The situation is not as though here is a person who has knowledge, and here is one without—like educated and uneducated. The opposite of wise is not ignorant—it is foolish. A foolish person may be highly intelligent and educated. He may have worldly wisdom but still be a fool. "The fool hath said in his heart, There is no God," Psalm 14:1 tells us. The person who does not have time for God in his life is a fool, according to the Book of Psalms. "The fool" has chosen the empty, vain, meaningless things, but the person in Christ, the wise man, has selected full, adequate, and meaningful things. That is the premise upon which Psalms approaches our lives.

In this psalm we have an accurate portrait of the truly happy man. "Blessed is the man" is an exclamation which specifically means, "O, how happy the man!" There is a tremendous intensity about it. The order of the Hebrew language in the sentence emphasizes the happiness. "O, how exceedingly happy is the man who does these things!"

Honestly, I cannot ever remember meeting a person who wanted to be unhappy. I know many unhappy people, but they dislike their unhappiness. Jesus summed it up, "I am come that they might have life, and that they might have it more abundantly!" (John 10:10). God wants us to be happy, fulfilled, blessed. It is amazing that what I desire the most in my heart, God wants me to experience. God is not a cosmic killjoy, not scheming how to make our lives miserable. He wants us to have whatever is good for us—satisfaction, meaning, and purpose in life.

I. The Character of the Happy Man

In these first three verses, the "blessed" man is described, and the last three contrast the blessed man with the "ungodly," the unhappy man. There is also the other side of the coin. Here is the happy man versus the unhappy man—the godly man versus the ungodly man, the wise man versus the foolish man.

Verse 1 treats *the conduct of this man.* "Blessed is the man that walketh not in the counsel of the ungodly, nor standeth in the way of sinners, nor sitteth in the seat of the scornful." The blessed person understands the importance of certain *negatives* in his life. So-called "positive thinking" goes only so far. If you want to be truly happy, you must "accentuate the" *negative,* not merely the positive. A wise person recognizes the significance of *not doing* certain things.

When I speak of "man" I do not think in terms of gender. Even in the Hebrew, man means mankind, humankind. Many times, in order to be happy, people think, do, or say things that are actually counterproductive and end up keeping themselves from being happy.

Here the psalmist emphasizes three negatives. First, the happy person is one who does not walk "in the counsel of the ungodly." He will not expose himself to the attitudes and ideas of "the ungodly." The word "ungodly" here is a general term in Hebrew denoting those who have no place for God in their lives. They are not necessarily "wicked" in the sense of gross sin, but they have no regard for God. The godly man cannot spend considerable time with those out of touch with God, except for discreet, Spirit-led witnessing.

The word "ungodly" emanates from a root meaning "unrest." The ungodly person has a profound restlessness in his soul. Deeply disturbed, he frantically scrambles for peace and satisfaction. The genuinely happy person does not seek advice and counsel from people outside of God. Imagine how many Christians allow unhappy people to tell them how to be happy! Don't let a loser tell you how to win. So many believers are susceptible even to the deceit of the so-called "New Age" movement. It is not "new" —such hogwash started with Lucifer in the garden of Eden. Verse 1 implies that we do not "hang around" an atmosphere where people have left God out. The happy person does not spend his time seeking advice from ungodly people.

Then the blessed person does not stand in the way of sinners. The word "sinners" means habitual rebels against God. Now it becomes worse. First, the ungodly referred to those who did not have a place for God in their lives. "Sinners" here points to those who habitually rebel against God. They are flagrantly determined to sin. The wise man will not spend his time in fellowship with such sinners.

Notice the possible digression. First of all, you have a man walking. That is harmless enough. All he does is walk—but then he stops. Then he sits, which may imply identification, and he joins them, as it were. Perhaps he started out just casually listening, certainly with no intent of following Satan's path. Then he stopped and found himself enjoying the company of rebels against God.

Then there is the phrase, "... nor sitteth in the seat of the scornful." If you walk with and stand with that kind of people, you may ultimately join their attitude toward God. The word "scornful" is bloodcurdling because it speaks of individuals who laugh at, ridicule, and sneer at God. This verse vividly deals with three steps away from God. First, they become careless in their contacts. They walk in areas where they should not walk, and engage in activities with ungodly people. Then the scenario worsens as they become involved with miscreants who laugh at and ridicule the very things of God.

This verse portrays for us the tragic downward path of one who associates with the wrong people and links his life with the wrong ideas of life. We should witness to those outside of Christ—by all means. That assignment is given to us, but we cannot draw our strength from people without God. The quickest way for us to become unhappy in our faith and to have our Christian joy diminished is to make our associations and attachments with ungodly people. Yes, the happy person knows there are limits to what he can do. Maybe some of you have lost your joy. One reason may be that you have become attached to people who have excluded God from their lives. There is certainly no happiness there.

Verse 1 spoke of the happy man's *conduct*, the things he should not do—his *character*. Then verse 2 deals with the things he should do, and I would call it:

II. The Communion of the Happy Man

This verse concerns what he dwells upon. "But his delight is in the law of the Lord; and in his law doth he meditate day and night." "The law of the Lord" refers to the Scriptures, the written Word of God. Throughout the Bible, "the law" refers not only to the Ten Commandments and the first five books—the Pentateuch— but in the Jewish mind had reference to the written Scriptures. Literally the verse goes: "in the law of the Lord is his delight." The emphasis here is on the Word of God. A happy man knows there are some things he must not do, but he is also aware of some things he must do.

The writer mentions two here. First, he *delights* in the Word of God. He did not consider the law to be a set of rigid restrictions that hampered and burdened him. To him the law was not troublesome and did not fetter him. Neither was the law a hard set of restraints squeezing the joy out of life. Rather, he found the Word of God a joy to his heart and a source of happiness to his heart and mind. He discovered it was wonderful to learn the Word of God and also to obey and do the Word. Jesus said: "My yoke is easy, and my burden is light" (Matt. 11:30). The happy person discovers that God's Word is a source of endless joy and blessing. It is food and drink for a hungry, thirsty soul.

Not only did he *delight* in the Word of God, but, second, *meditated* upon it. He filled his heart and mind with the Word. It is a tragedy when people claim to love the Lord and yet cannot tell you whether Deuteronomy is in the Old or New Testament. Many even think there is a Book of Hezekiah! I even heard one politician who, trying to make an impression on religious folks, called Deuteronomy one of the apostles! We are to fix our minds on the Word, which is a lamp unto our feet and a light unto our path (see Ps. 119:105). It is not difficult.

The word "meditate" is an interesting word. It means to "moan." Black believers know how to moan. Mmmmmmmm. The word could be translated "hum." Devout Jews know how to moan. Go to the "Wailing Wall" in Jerusalem, and you can't understand a word they say. They are sort of talking to themselves, moaning and humming, repeating the Torah, the Law. That is the kind of description we have here.

The happy man is characterized by hiding God's Word in his heart and uttering that Word to himself and others. This is a rather common comparison, but it reminds me of a cow chewing its cud. That cow never seems to be in a hurry but continually chews that same old cud. The cow chews it again and again, savoring it. That is part of the process of rumination. Meditation on the Word of God is spiritual rumination, bringing the Word up and chewing on it, tasting it. Think on it, moan it, hum it, repeat it. The happy individual does that. I am not talking about some sort of religious nut or some imbalanced fanatic who is giving too much emphasis to the spiritual. I have in mind a person who bubbles over to the extent he may shout "wow!" The happy man's *communion*.

Then verse 3 treats:

III. The Condition of the Happy Man

"He shall be like a tree planted by the rivers of water, that bringeth forth his fruit in his season; his leaf also shall not wither; and whatsoever he doeth shall prosper." This makes two statements about the condition of the truly happy man. First, he is like a *tree planted*. The tree here is rooted and grounded securely in the earth. It speaks of stability and strength. When all the storms rage, when the blistering heat of summer bakes us, when the burning winds of the desert blow, when the drought blights and water is rare—the happy man's roots go deep, and he is planted by rivers of water. Winds of change and upheaval cannot detour or root up the blessed person. This forcefully speaks of fruitfulness and vigor, and this fortification is found throughout the Word of God.

Give attention to the prophet Jeremiah: "Blessed is the man that trusteth in the Lord, and whose hope the Lord is. For he shall be as a tree planted by the waters, that spreadeth out her roots by the river, and shall not see when heat cometh, but her leaf shall be green; and shall not be careful in the year of drought, neither shall cease from yielding fruit" (Jer. 17:7-8). Jeremiah had the same insight as the psalmist. All of the elements of the world cannot affect the fact that his roots are deep, and his strength is sufficient. This verse also tells us he is like a *tree prospering*: the tree "bringeth forth his fruit in his season; his leaf also shall not wither; and whatsoever he doeth shall prosper."

We will miss the point if we try to apply these three verses to what is today called prosperity. The main point here is not material but spiritual productivity—a fruitful, a prosperous tree, producing that which is worthwhile. His life blesses others and is an inspiration to them. His deep roots are strengthened in the hour of testing and are watered by the Word of God that will be a source of his strength and of the stability of his life.

A tree in the Middle East is prized because most of the land is desert and basically barren. A tree like this would be a veritable oasis in the desert, standing out like a sentinel. Here, in the midst of devastation, is a tree, branches spreading toward the sky. Even the intense heat and the torrid desert siroccos cannot wither its leaf or cause its fruit to fail from producing—and that is what God intends for His people to be.

Verse 4 launches into:

IV. The Contrast to the Happy Man

What a contrast it is. "The ungodly are not so. . . . " This is a very brief transition. The contrast is so brief we are prone to think— *Well, why doesn't he go into more detail?* The brevity of this contrast magnifies the difference in these two people. Here is perhaps the greatest contrast in the entire Bible. In the New Testament, for instance, there is the contrast between the wheat and the tares. The wheat is likened unto God's children; the tares, to the ungodly. There is also contrast between the sheep and the goats. The sheep are likened unto God's people; the goats, to the ungodly. Try to keep the flourishing tree in your mind. "The ungodly are not so."

What are they like? The ungodly "are like the chaff which the wind driveth away." The chaff is the hull, the waste material, of the grain. The grain is encased in a hull, a leafy material. When farmers would harvest the grain they would spread it onto the threshing floors. Threshing floors were nearly always on the crest of a hill. Even today the process is the same. Israeli growers throw the grain onto the threshing floor, trample it to separate the grain from the chaff or hull, and, then with a shovel or a rake, throw it into the air, where the wind blowing across these hilltops will carry the chaff away, and the grain will fall back to the floor. Finally, all the chaff is blown away, and only the grain remains. Then they use the grain and are blessed by it.

There is nothing much more worthless than chaff. Whatever chaff was left on the floor would be piled up and burned. At threshing time the atmosphere would be filled with the tiny particles of chaff. You will remember that Jesus talked of the man who was concerned about the mote in his brother's eye. The mote was perhaps a little piece of chaff that irritated one's eye. It was a nuisance. Nothing is more worthless than chaff. The contrast is evident.

The godly man is like this tree—sturdy, strong, fruitful, with verdant foliage. The ungodly man is like chaff—worthless, useless, dead, dry, helpless, hopeless. What a contrast. Doom is inevitable; the wind will drive it away. The ungodly person is like a house build on the sand. When the winds and rains come, it will fall (see Matt. 7:26-27). Contrasted to the happy man is the person who has no room for God in his life.

Job had another vivid description along these lines. Job described streams in the desert and the people who live like those streams.

My brethren have dealt deceitfully as a brook, and as the stream of brooks they pass away; Which are blackish by reason of the ice, and wherein the snow is hid: What time they wax warm, they vanish: when it is hot, they are consumed out of their place (Job 6:15-17).

Those streams wound out into the desert where the intense heat dried up the water. Those who followed those streams perished. Notice also verse 18: "The paths of their way are turned aside; they go to nothing, and perish." Worthless. What a picture of those without God. That comparison, like the chaff, highlighted individuals who thought they could handle life apart from God—without obeying God, without delighting in the things of God. They went their own way; they didn't want to be bothered by God. They thought they were going to have happiness, but God's Word verifies that their end was destruction and doom, and their lives were destined to be worthless. What a vivid contrast with a healthy tree!

Verse 5 makes it plain that the ungodly person is under condemnation. "Therefore the ungodly shall not stand in the judgment, nor sinners in the congregation of the righteous." Two facts are stated here. The writer was not saying that the ungodly person will not appear at the judgment. He will definitely appear, but the phrase "shall not stand" literally means "shall not maintain himself." In other words, he will not survive the judgment. He will stand before God without excuse and defense. The ungodly will stand before God, and will be condemned without reprieve. There is no mercy for the person who lives without God. Flimsy excuses and pious rhetoric will not help in the judgment.

But the verse also declares: ". . . nor sinners in the congregation of the righteous." That has puzzled many interpreters. To me this is rather clear. In every congregation there are hypocrites who try to act the part but whose hearts are not committed to the Lord. Pretenders. Play actors. We cannot look into hearts. It is neither for you nor me to judge. In the final judgment, sinners will not be able to identify with the congregation of the righteous. The genuine heart condition of an individual will be manifest in the judgment. People *know what* we do. God *knows why* we do it. Here is a solemn warning to the person who thinks he can associate with godly people, and that is all God requires. What God requires is a heart that is turned toward Him and a life under His control. Even though it is commendable to surround ourselves with Christian people, what matters most of all is committing our lives to the Lord. At the final judgment sinners will not be in the congregation of the righteous—no goats with the sheep; no chaff with the flourishing, vibrant trees of God.

"The Lord knows the way of the righteous: but the way of the ungodly shall perish." The person who excludes God from his life—whatever else he may think, whatever else he may do—is headed inevitably toward destruction. No good conclusion can come from that kind of life. There is inevitable separation from God. You can "be sure your sin will find you out" (Num. 32:23). "The soul that sinneth, it shall die" (Ezek. 18:4,20). Don't be deceived, God is not mocked. What a man sows, that he will reap (see Gal. 6:7). The end result of a life lived without God is eternal hell.

Notice the Psalmist's conclusion about the righteous, a contrast that is beautiful. "The Lord knoweth the way of the righteous." The word "know" here means more than that God is simply informed or merely aware. The core of this message is: God cares about the righteous! The word "knoweth" is in a Hebrew tense that speaks of continuous action. God is continually watching over the way of the righteous. The way of the godly is one watched by, guarded by, approved by, and blessed by God.

Isn't that wonderful to know? God watches our lives. When we cry out through our experiences—and devastating things happen to all of us—God cares deeply. In the midst of every experience, as you cry out to God, sometimes you cry in bewilderment, sometimes in doubt, sometimes in fear. You may cry from discouragement and despair. There may be happiness, or there may be sadness. There may be any number of experiences, but through those experiences of life we reach out for God, and He is there!

The truly happy person is one who recognizes there are some things he can't do. He can't associate with people who, however innocent they may appear, have no contact with God. He will not associate and link his life with those who are habitual sinners and those who laugh at and ridicule the things of God. Rather, he will spend his life delighting in the law of the Lord, meditating upon it, letting it express itself in his life. And he will be like a tree—tall, sturdy, flourishing—planted by rivers of water. But the person who has no time for God is like chaff—dry, dead, worthless trash—no hope for him, only the wind driving him away to be burned, to be swept away without hope! "The Lord knoweth the way of the righteous, but the way of the ungodly will perish." What a tremendous source of strength and blessing. How deep and immense should be our total commitment to God!

2
Reaching Your Full Potential

Psalm 8

The second most important question that has ever been asked is confronted in this psalm. The most important question is: "What think ye of Christ?" (Matt. 22:42*a*) That is the basic question of life for all of us. Until you properly answer that question, none of the others matter. What one does with Jesus Christ is the bedrock, foundational question, and pursuit in every person's heart.

The second most important question is found in verse 4 of this psalm. "What is man, that thou art mindful of him? and the son of man that thou visitest him?" Who am I? What did God make me to be? What kind of being is man? Charles Darwin postulated that man is merely a highly developed animal. Is that what man is? Sigmund Freud's concept was that man was just an underdeveloped child. Karl Marx stated that man is basically an economic factor in the world. Isaiah, pooling the collective wisdom of mankind, wrote that all men are like grass, and he magnified the temporary nature of man on this earth, that we are passing away.

Is there an answer to the riddle of mankind? What is man? What is the "son of man" that God visits him or that God is concerned for him?

Whatever answer mankind may give to the question—What is man?—God is the only one who has the right answer. Psalm 8 presents God's answer to the riddle of mankind—the question, What is man? God answers and asserts that He created us to be kings, to have dominion, to have authority. He fashioned mankind as the apex, the climax, the crowning achievement of His creative genius. Man was created by God, but the problem is that we don't act like royalty. Our crowns have become tarnished. In fact, history demonstrates that we act more like slaves than sovereigns, more like knaves than kings. What happened? People through the ages have remarked, "I don't understand why God created mankind the way it is." Here's the truth: God didn't create mankind the way it is.

God created only two people, and He was perfectly delighted with them. He saw that His work was "good" and "very good." What we look aghast at today is not mankind as God created it but mankind as sin has made it, has dethroned him, has debased him, and defiled him. So the perfect image God had in His heart for mankind was before sin entered into human experience. God created mankind for dominion (v. 6), to have authority, to be "crowned... with glory and honor" (v. 5). Man lost the royal nature that was in him. How can we restore that position? How does one recapture what God intended one to be? How do you live up to your full potential, reach that possibility God has desired for you?

Within every person's heart, is an emptiness, a deep-down hunger that is filled only in God. Only as God is given liberty to move into our lives do we ever begin to reach our intended potential. Does or can an individual ever become what God created him to be and what he in his heart longs to be? This psalm answers the question (v. 1). The first point and the last point are the same. The first point I call *God's praise* (v. 1). The last point is *God's position* (v. 9).

I. God's Praise

These verses open and close the same: "O Lord our Lord, how excellent is thy name in all the earth!" Many call this an "envelope psalm." It starts and finishes the same way, and the truth is wrapped up in between. Come to the end, and you reach the start. The psalm goes on in an eternal cycle of emphasis on the glorious excellence of God's name. Here is the praise of the Lord God. It is almost as if the psalmist were unable to express God's glory, and all he could do was add an exclamation point. Sometimes it appears that the name of God is not acknowledged in all the earth, but His name is indeed acknowledged as excellent in the hearts of all of those who have known Him.

There are millions of Muslims who claim Allah as their god. There are millions of Buddhists who bow before altars and shrines to Buddha. There are millions of Hindus who grovel before myriads of idols. There are still millions of communists and atheists who claim there is no God, and yet there are countless millions of others who testify with their words that God exists but who live as if He does not. In spite of how people ignore the reality of God, the truth is that the name of God is majestic and excellent in all of the earth.

All across the world, millions claim the name of Jehovah God of the Old Testament. Emmanuel ("God with us") is the name He was given in the New Testament (Matt. 1:23). Jesus ("Jehovah is salvation") is Immanuel, and the whole creation is full of His glory. There is no place where God is not. He is omnipresent. Everywhere He is seen. Many people argue, "I don't see him. Many others don't see Him." Let it be understood: you can never, with rational processes, understand God, but when you come to Him with faith, He is perfectly understandable, but only through faith in Christ. You can never, with reasoning, ascertain the veracity of the Word of God, but when you approach it with faith, it reveals itself to be absolutely truth. You see what you want to see.

If you choose to receive Christ in faith, that is your choice. If you choose to doubt, that is also your choice. A major problem is that many people who attend church say, "Prove Yourself to me, God." In doubt, they demand that God prove Himself to them. If that is your selfish desire, God will never do it. Remember Jesus' account of the rich man and Lazarus (see Luke 16:19-31). They both died, and the rich man went to hell. In torment he lifted up his eyes, and he saw Lazarus in Abraham's bosom, and he cried, "I'm tormented in this flame, Father Abraham; Let Lazarus dip his finger in water and put a drop of water on my tongue, for I am tormented in this flame" (v. 24, Author). That was not possible because of the "great gulf" (v. 26), the wide chasm, between them, and so the rich man had another idea.

"I have five brothers back on earth. Send somebody, even send Lazarus, back to tell them so they won't come to this place." Remember Abraham's solemn reply, "They have Moses and the prophets; let them hear them. If they won't believe them, they won't believe even if someone is raised from the dead" (vv. 29-31, Author).

God is not God because He performs miracles that convince us He is God. He is not God because we believe Him to be God. He is not God because we trust Him to be God. He is God whether or not we believe in Him. Our faith does not make Him God. But unless you choose to approach Him with faith, it doesn't make a bit of difference what else may occur. You still won't believe Him.

You believe what you choose to believe, either coming with faith or doubt, with faith or skepticism. It is your choice. We can neither explain it nor understand it. In the world most people do not claim the name of God, and live and act as if God doesn't exist. But in spite of the world's infidelity—"O Lord our Lord, how excellent is thy name, in all the earth!" He is there. He is here.

The key is: *Our Lord.* He is not merely God in a detached manner. He is *my* Lord, *my* God. The truth of the Word of God is not simply that there is a theology or a philosophy that claims there is a God who somewhere and somehow exists, but the verity of the Word is that the Lord of all the universe, the mystery and infinitude of eternity, is the God who is *my* God. Here is the Lord's praise. "O Lord, . . . how excellent is thy name in all the earth! who hast set thy glory above the heavens." The heavens cannot contain the glory of God. God had to put it above the heavens.

Gaze into the vastness of outer space. Month after month astronomers discover new galaxies and stars. Christian scientists believe that God is still expanding His universe. Yet if they could reach to the end of all the innumerable galaxies of the universe, it is still too small to contain the glory of God above the heavens. When you focus the eyes of the heart upon the glory of God, the majesty of God; when you begin to comprehend who God is and begin to praise Him, it pinpoints an entirely new light upon life every day. The psalmist starts out with the Lord's praise. In verses 2 and 3, he extols:

II. The Lord's Power

In the Lord's name there is a superabundance of majesty. The name of the Lord is majestic, awesome, powerful. And the psalmist speaks initially about the name of the Lord as being a mighty conqueror. In verse 2 he declares that when his accusers, his avengers, his enemies try to attack God, "Out of the mouth of babes and sucklings thou hast ordained strength." God Himself asserts, "My glory is so powerful, My nature so strong that when all the might of an evil world marshals its forces to discredit, attack, and condemn Me, just the praise in the mouth of a baby is sufficient to sustain that strength in the world." The cry of a little infant is all the defense that God needs. The mere fact that we can conceive of God and from our earliest years we can express a desire for God, is convincing evidence of God. God is such a conqueror that the words of children carry far greater weight than all the accusations of mighty men.

In other words, you do not have to defend God, just as you don't have to defend an African lion against a domesticated tabby cat. You do not have to defend God—just praise Him. Acclaim God. Embrace, God, even as children do. It is interesting. Do you remember who the hero of the New Testament is? Really? A little child. "Except ye, . . . become as little children," Jesus put it, "ye shall not enter into the kingdom of heaven" (Matt. 18:3). He didn't teach that you had to become like the apostles Paul or Peter or John. He taught here how you make it to heaven; become like a little child. We refer to childlike faith—simple trust. A little child is the prime example of faith. The glory, the strength, the power, and the might of God are declared more clearly through simple, childlike faith than any other way—trusting in Him.

Then God is described as the mighty Creator, for the psalmist says, "When I consider your heavens, the work of your fingers, the moon and the stars, which you have set in place, what is man that you are mindful of him, . . . that you care for him?" (vv. 3-4, NIV) Here is a word concerning meditation. He testifies: "When I look at the stars and contemplate the heavens I think of how great all of that is and how insignificant we are." He is absolutely awestricken and smitten. He reflects on God as the mighty Creator.

Since David was a shepherd, I have an idea he was most familiar with the stars. Many a "starry, starry night" he sat on a hillside and stared at the heavens. Perhaps he knew the names of certain stars and galaxies. Maybe he was able to remember the positions of the stars during certain times of the year. Out in the grazing land at night, what else could he do but sing, play the harp, and be star-struck? He was overwhelmed by the majesty and the mystery of God. He was awestricken by it all.

His awe should be totally eclipsed by ours. We know inestimably more about the vastness of the universe and the intricate nature of all there is. As we consider God, the mighty Creator, it is all a tribute to His power. In fact, the psalmist indicates it is God's finger. Now, you know, that means it is "no big deal" with God. The Bible speaks of the arm of God, the hand of God, and the finger of God. An arm is more powerful than a finger. A hand is more powerful than one finger. All God had to do was speak, and the worlds were flung into existence.

Using an illustration we could all understand, the singer observed, "When I look at all the heavens, when I consider the sun, the moon, the stars, all there is—when I think of it all, I realize it was done by the finger of God." God just did it. The "Great Creator" is also our Savior. He sings to us of the Lord's power.

Then, beginning in verse 4 (this is really the heart of the passage) he speaks of:

III. The Lord's Passion

All of us have our lives guided by some passion, a force which drives us. Maybe it is a passion to achieve, or a passion to experience; but we are pushed by a passion. What pushes God? What drives God? What is the motivating force of God? Here it is delineated clearly in three ways. These stanzas tell us that God's passion, first of all, is expressed in *His coming to us*. "What is man that you think about him and that you even care to visit him?" It is expressed in *His caring for us*. The word "visit" means to be concerned for. Who are we that God would care anything about us? So His passion is seen by His concern for us, His caring for us. Finally, it is revealed in *His crowning us*. "[He] crowned [man] with glory and with honor." These are the passions that drive God—to come to us, to care for us, to crown us.

First, the psalmist notes as God comes to us, what is man? You're mindful of him? The son of man that You visit him? Think about it. God is mindful of us. Wonderful. God is more interested in people than planets. God is more concerned about souls than stars. God cares more about us than the universe. The God of the telescope is also the God of the microscope. The God of the vastness of space is also the God of the specific reaches of my spirit.

A little girl prayed the Model Prayer, and as she prayed she talked about God "knowing my name." She didn't understand how it was phrased, but she prayed to a God in heaven who knows her name. God knows your name and who you are. God is mindful of you. The glory of God is not seen in dynamic, spectacular events, or in the intricate details of the universe. The glory of God is seen in that He comes to us. He wants to live in us, to indwell our lives, and the intriguing fact we see at this point is found in the words for mankind in verse 4. Two different Hebrew words are used. The first one is the Hebrew word *enosh*, and it simply means mortal man, man in his weakness.

What is mortal man? What is weak, puny, sinful, helpless little man that you would think of him? In our weakness, in our helplessness, God cares for us and loves us. God is interested in us. God comes to us in our weakness, and it is magnified as you reach the second half of that verse. He says, "What is . . . the son of man?" (In the Hebrew the word "man" here is the word "adama," from which we receive our word "Adam," meaning dust). There is no definite article there—literally the Hebrew does not ask what is *the son of man?* but what is *son of man?* What is son of dust?

This is a phrase used without the definite article over one hundred times in the Old Testament, and it always means, "What is man as a descendant of Adam—just plain, puny, nameless man?" Yet God cares about insignificant, helpless, poor, weak you and me. There is the passion of God. He comes to us.

In the New Testament, however, the phrase is changed. The phrase, "the Son of man," does have the definite article with it, and it always refers to Jesus. The usage is a vivid illustration that we only become the individuals God wants us to be through Jesus Christ.

What were you intended to be? "Turn your eyes upon Jesus." He is King of kings and Lord of lords. Revelation exults: He has made us to be "kings and priests [forever with Him]" (5:10). So Jesus is the epitome, the description, the example of what we are intended to be.

The word "visitest" in verse 4 means to care. What are we that

God would care about us? Why would the omnipotent God of the universe care about our hurts, our confusion, our intense pressure? Why should God concern Himself? And then God crowns us. This psalm goes on to indicate that God has made man to be a "little lower than the angels" (v. 5), slightly less than the angels. God has crowned us with glory and honor. God has made us to have dominion over the works of His hands and has put all things under our feet.

How breathtaking! God invested us with the dignity second only to His own, second only to the very nature of Himself. God made us to be rulers over the world that He created. What a high position, what lofty dignity God gives to mankind. It is as though, the psalmist said, God set a regal crown upon man's head, a scepter in his hand, and a robe of royalty around his shoulders. It is a crown of glory and honor. Nowhere is human dignity more clearly and boldly asserted than in this passage. God intended for us to be regal.

Before the fall in the Garden of Eden, when God created Adam and Eve, that is how He wants us to be. If you want to understand the full impact of this psalm, turn to Hebrews 2. The writer of Hebrews quotes this psalm, verses 4 and following. Hebrews speaks in detail about this and declares that God has "put all things in subjection under [him]." Nothing was left out, but key on the last portion of verse 8. "But now we see not yet all things put under him."

Mankind botched it up. Sin entered into human experience, and we have not achieved what God intended for us. The intent of Hebrews 2 is to display before us the high and lofty ideal God had for mankind and to show us that, in Christ, we can indeed reach our full potential. It is all found in our Lord and Savior. We become what God created us to become in Jesus Christ. He restores the dominion, the authority, the dignity that sin snatched away. Jesus Christ makes us to be what God created us to be.

Though we may not seem to be rulers and kings with honor in this life, we discover in Revelation 1:5-6 that God has "redeemed us through the blood of the Lamb and has made us to be kings and priests, and we shall live and reign with Him for ever and ever" (author's words). Our fullest potential and our utmost fulfillment is found through Jesus Christ.

People were meant to have dominion, but by no means do they have dominion. We are creatures frustrated by our circumstances, defeated by our temptations, conscious of our weaknesses. We stagger with an albatross around our necks. We should be free, but we are bound. We should be kings, but we are slaves. Now whatever else is true and whatever else may not be true, one crushing reality is certain—people are not what they were meant to be. You and I are not what we were meant to be. How, then, do we realize our potential? How do we fill the longing in our hearts? How do we deal with the inadequacies of our spirits? How do we realize the tremendous possibilities that lie within us? Only in and through Jesus Christ. That is the impact of Hebrews 2.

After writing about what God intended and how God created us—also how we do not yet see all things put under him—the psalmist turned to human failure. In spite of what mankind is, in spite of his abject failure, in spite of the fact man has not realized his full potential, and that man is not where God intended for him to be—"We see Jesus, who was made a little lower than the angels for the suffering of death, crowned with glory and honor; that he, by the grace of God should taste death for every man" (v. 9). It is not necessary for us to be separated from God, to spend eternity apart from God, to remain incomplete.

Jesus tasted death for all of us without exception. "For it became him [Jesus], for whom are all things, and by whom are all things, in bringing many sons unto glory" (v. 10). That is magnificent. God is in the divine process of doing exactly that. He is bringing many children to glory—from all over the world, "every kindred, every tribe." That is the whole purpose of the gospel. That is the redemptive nature of the Word of God. Those who come to Jesus Christ, He is now in the process of bringing to glory through His death on that cross. God said, "[I made you] a little lower than the angels" not a little higher than the animals. Perverted, incomplete human science calls us animals, and unregenerate people often live like vicious animals. What a degrading view of man! They claim that man is just an educated animal. God said, "No, you're not just an efficient animal, but I have created you in My image, in My likeness. I created you for dominion, for authority. I created you to be a king."

Humans spend their lives grabbing for the illusive dream, stretching toward "just one more high," one more achievement, one more experience, and then they feel, "I'll reach that satisfaction my heart longs for." But that never happens. It reminds us of that old song, "I'm Always Chasing Rainbows." Our goals are illusive and gone, and there is still an emptiness and uncertainty. Many spend their lives like someone throwing an empty bucket into an empty well and grow old drawing nothing up. That was never God's intention. God intended for us to have dominion and authority—kings crowned with glory and honor. God comes to us, cares for us, and crowns us. And we are crowned, not through any human merit of our own, but we are crowned when we are possessed by the Lord and He makes out of our lives what we could never make of ourselves.

And the psalm ends with:

IV. The Lord's Position

He repeats the same phrase that captured us at the beginning. "O Lord our Lord, how excellent is they name in all the earth!" The skeptic protests, "Prove it. Prove it. How's God's name excellent in all the earth?" In this psalm the singer has given us two reasons. Let me summarize them. First, he has presented us with *the reason of God's greatness*. When I contemplate the heavens—the sun, the moon, the stars—and consider that You created them with only Your finger, the power and greatness of God proclaims the excellency of His name.

But, more than that, the psalmist asserts that we prove it by considering God's grace. God's grandeur is obvious to anyone who has the eyes to see it. God's grace. How amazing that grace is. How marvelous. How wonderful. The God who can orbit the Milky Way and then take a hundred million galaxies in the palm of His hand and toss them into space like a handful of stardust—that God loves us, cares for us, has grace to give us! I know His name is excellent because of His grace.

But if you still want to argue, the psalmist says, "O Lord our Lord, how excellent is they name in all the earth!" That is the beginning and the end of this psalm. The psalm begins where it ends; it ends where it begins, and it moves through a cycle endlessly, eternally. "O Lord our Lord, how excellent is they name . . ." Living for His glory, possessed by His Spirit, we're on our way to glory. The Captain of our salvation who was "made perfect through sufferings" is "bringing many sons unto glory."

Someday we shall indeed be kings and queens and shall rule with Him forever. This was all in His plan. All we were intended to be and all that we shall be is in Jesus Christ. That is why we obey Him, why we publicly profess Him, why we are baptized as believers, why we band together in churches to worship Him, why we pool our strength and resources to reach the ends of the earth with His message of salvation.

We live to honor Him. From our hearts we cry, "O Lord our Lord, . . ." It is marvelous. "He's our Lord, our Friend," is a magnificent expression.

But is He your Lord? Whether or not you claim Him as Lord doesn't make Him Lord or keep Him from being Lord. He is Lord, regardless, but the key to your realizing your potential is when, with an open heart, you can testify, "O Lord our Lord [My Lord] how excellent is thy name in all the earth!"

3
The Life That Excels

Psalm 36

This psalm contrasts human wickedness at its worst and divine goodness at its best, between what people claim will make you happy and what God affirms will make you happy. People strive to achieve with the expectation that accomplishments will bestow satisfaction or meaning to their lives.

Innumerable voices are clamoring to convey their message of what it takes to attain the life that excels. What kind of life is that? I candidly believe that God would not give us a desire that was not attainable. He does not play games with us. If God implants a yearning in my heart to be satisfied and to experience joy, then that very fact indicates I can achieve it.

How can you find the truly satisfying, fulfilling life? Let's discover the answer in the three major divisions of this psalm. First, this psalm asserts that the life that excels views:

I. The Futility of Sin

Those who give themselves to the life-style of Satan do so with the expectation they will somehow have meaning. The Bible makes it plain that when disobedience toward God and rebellion become one's norm and pattern for life, then that person has given himself, not to satisfaction but to futility. Wickedness and transgression make a person miss the opportunity to find meaning and purpose in life. What one believes will determine what one does. Whatever your creed is (and we all have a creed) will determine how you act.

In these first four verses we see that sin has convinced this man to adopt a false creed, and he has pushed God out of his life. This is seen in two ways: first, in his attitude: "The transgression of the wicked saith within my heart that there is no fear of God before his eyes. For he flattereth himself in his own eyes, until his iniquity be found to be hateful" (vv. 1-2). His attitude is one of rebellion and arrogance toward God.

The phrase, "the transgression of the wicked," could be translated "the oracle of transgression," and plainly means that transgression is his god. He worships evil and sin. "Transgression" is the normal Hebrew word for rebellion, and here's the picture. In the heart of the believer, God is enshrined as his authority. To him, what God says becomes his obedient act and response. But these two verses describe a man who enthroned wickedness as his authority. Rebellion had the same place that the believer grants to God. He had become convinced that God was irrelevant to his life. He thought God was not going to catch him in his sin. "The transgression of the wicked *saith* within my heart" (Author's italics). The word "saith" is a forceful word, and it is always employed in the Hebrew concerning the sayings of God. In the Old Testament where you read "thus saith the Lord," that is the word used here. There is a fixed contract in the believer's mind—"Thus saith the Lord."

God speaks. He is to be obeyed, to be loved, and to be enshrined in our hearts. In the sinner's life, though, the devil says, "Wickedness is to be enshrined and to be obeyed. Rebellion should dictate the pattern of life." The wicked person has pushed God away from his life, and "there is no fear of God before his eyes." That speaks of sheer arrogance toward God.

That attitude is absolutely foolish for there is a God, and there are biblical absolutes. These standards are true. When we disregard these standards, we will not escape the judgment springing from violating them. This man assumed that God somehow was not going to interfere with his life. That is folly. This wicked man had made his own evil desires and perverse tendencies a god in his life. Today's society, notably in America and the Western world, has abandoned the Bible and the God of the Bible, bypassing the standards of the Word. Our world has forsaken these absolute principles. There is something called right and something called wrong. What we are reaping in America is the payment for our infatuation with sinful man's ideas and ideals, resulting in chaos. The moral breakdown in our day will mean that one out of ten of us can expect to spend time in a mental hospital.

People have disregarded God's Word to the extent we face an AIDS epidemic of worldwide proportions. We are anticipating at least 270,000 known cases of AIDS as this book goes to press. At that rate, if we multiply that by ten years, over 250 million people will be destroyed. That is the entire population of America! Man's rebellious ideas make God seem irrelevant, and our arrogant attitude toward Him is an effort of sinful people to discover meaning and purpose. It is a frantic rat race.

The psalmist writes that the life which excels understands that man's way is futile. Sinful human concepts will not work. The excelling life deals with *attitudes*, and also with *actions*. The words of the wicked person are iniquity and deceit. He has left off wisdom and goodness. One translation states that he ceases to act circumspectly and to do good. He devises mischief upon his bed and lies awake at night thinking of filthy devices. He has no sense of ethics or morality.

His attitude was disruptive because it did not allow for God in his life. He acted upon his sinful mind-set. One's attitude of independence from God will soon express itself in one's activity. Note the text declares that his words were "iniquity and deceit." One who rejects absolute moral standards will see nothing wrong with lying. Lying in high and low places results from rebellion and irreverence toward God. People will look you right in the eyes and lie to you.

When one does not have a God to whom one is accountable, one's mouth will be filled with iniquity and deceit. Recently a friend sent me a page out of a professional journal. In a survey of fifty-two major corporations in America, over 50 percent of the executives confessed that, if it meant their "getting ahead," they would lie in word and deed. That is amazing! And sometimes it is no better in church, is it? Professing Christians may even lie to one another. Sinful man suggests, "Do your own thing, and you'll achieve your goals without God," but with that attitude, the deep goals of life will never be achieved.

Sin and rebellion will not make it. Now this man had deteriorated badly. Once he had acted right, but no more. Once he probably felt that God had certain claims on his life, but now he was living as though God were nowhere. He lay awake at night scheming evil. He was not suddenly overtaken with temptation—he was meticulously plotting his sinful activity.

"He abhorreth not evil" (v. 4). The word "evil" in Hebrew means "to break up that which is good." It is close to the Hebrew equivalent to the Greek word *pornē* (whore) from which we derive *pornography* (the writings of a whore). It means vulgarity, lewdness, depravity, and corruption. This man once knew to do right, but now he lay in bed conjuring up filth. When one goes away from God there is nothing one won't do. We wonder how people who once professed faith in God can be caught in gross sin and still seem not to care about God.

When one listens to the voice of Satan instead of God, one will daydream and "nightdream" on dirt. You argue, "I wouldn't." Yes, you would. Ignore God, and you can find yourself in this man's shoes. This man's persistent pursuit of evil had resulted in deceitful words and diabolical deeds. Such is a dead-end street. If you yearn for a life that excels, you must understand that sin is futile. It offers nothing deeply satisfying or enduring. How well the saints of God recognized the emptiness of sin. "Moses, . . . refused to be called the son of Pharaoh's daughter. Choosing rather to suffer affliction with the people of God, than to enjoy the pleasures of sin for a season" (Heb. 11:24-25). Young Joseph rejected the sexual advances of Potiphar's wife, was falsely imprisoned for his stand, and yet ended up second only to Pharaoh Himself (see Gen. 39:1 to 41:47). And think of young Daniel who "purposed in his heart that he would not defile himself" (Dan. 1:8*a*). They were aware of *the futility of sin*.

Second, this passage reminds us that the life that excels sees:

II. The Fullness of Salvation

The psalmist then launched into the attributes of God—the mercy, the faithfulness, the righteousness, and the judgment of God. The psalmist wrote: "Thy mercy, O Lord, is in the heavens" (v. 5*a*). How immense are the heavens? We do not know. God is still unfolding His universe. The mercy of God is limitless; His blessings are inexhaustible. "Thy faithfulness reacheth unto the clouds. Thy righteousness is like the great mountains" (vv. 5 *b*-6*a*). A mountain portrays stability and strength. We can count on the rock-like righteousness of God.

"Thy judgments are a great deep: O Lord, thou preserveth man and beast" (v. 6b). There are parts of the ocean that seem fathomless. The Marianna Trench in the South Pacific is 36,198 feet deep—nearly seven miles, but there could be places that are deeper. There is a picture of God's sufficiency and also His profundity. In contrast is human fickleness and shallowness. God's provisions are inexhaustible. When you seek the life that excels, you begin to understand the sufficiency of God's salvation. God's love is matchless. It's as high as the heavens, as immovable as the mountains, as deep and inexhaustible as the oceans. So he describes salvation as *sufficient*. Then he refers to it as a *shelter*.

"How excellent is thy lovingkindness, O God! therefore the children of men put their trust under the shadow of thy wings" (v. 7). Here you would expect that he used the convenient name for God, Jehovah, the name of God in relation to Israel. The word for *Lord* in verse 7 is Elohim, the name of God as Creator. He was making the point that God is faithful to all people, not merely to Israel. You can trust the God of creation; He will do what He has pledged to do.

Several times God's Word employs the metaphor of wings to refer to God. Jesus spoke of being sheltered by wings as He stood on the Mount of Olives and wept over the city of Jerusalem. "How often would I have gathered thy children together, even as a hen gathereth her chickens under her wings, and ye would not" (Matt. 23:37). View in your mind a cold night as a hen gathers her chicks and pulls them underneath her wings. For those chicks, the safest shelter in the world is under their mother's wings. How infinitely more secure you are when sheltered under the wings of the Almighty God.

Then the singer wrote of *satisfaction*. Speaking of the fullness of salvation, he has described it in terms of *sufficiency, shelter,* and now *satisfaction*. Verses 8 and 9 are magnificent. This flies in the face of all the world tells us about God. "They shall be abundantly satisfied with the fatness of thy house; and thou shalt make them drink of the river of thy pleasure. For with thee is the fountain of life: in thy light shall we see light." The Word of God declares that God gives satisfaction. He provides an abundance. What we usually hear, though, is, "Well, it's tough down here. Things just go from bad to worse. But someday, someday it's going to be better. We're going to be with Him someday and He will make up, He will compensate for all the things we've had to experience down here. There will be pie in the sky someday."

It is a fact that they who life godly lives will suffer persecution. It is also true that many times saintly, godly people do not receive the recognition they deserve. They often do not have the social status and standing that worldly people have. In spite of this, I emphasize that God never gives anything inferior. God's measuring stick is different from the world's. Many Americans are so shallow they think life should be judged by bank accounts, securities, cars, real estate, appearance, and human clout. But those are foolish human standards. All those things have this in common: they will not last. God has never promised you those things. What He does promise you is real, excellent.

"They shall be abundantly satisfied with the fatness of thy house; and thou shalt make them drink of the river of thy pleasures" (v. 8). The word "pleasures" here is *edena*. Sounds like Eden, doesn't it? It connotes the delights and pleasures God gave Adam and Eve in the perfection of the Garden of Eden. He wants to restore to us believers the pleasures of Eden.

Genuine pleasure is God's invention. Satan has never invented any real pleasure. Satan is a loser from the beginning. He has never had an original thought. He is the original plagiarizer. What is sin? sin is not necessarily doing something that in itself is wrong. Sin is taking something God intended to be used in one way and perverting and abusing it, using it in the wrong way. Now that's sin. It is the perversion of good. Satan doesn't even have enough sense to think up something evil in the way of pleasure. He just grabs something good and messes it up. God is the inventor of genuine pleasure. You can become wonderfully satisfied in the Lord. God is not against pleasure—He is against the fleeting, unfulfilling "pleasures" Satan offers. God is not merely going to give you pleasures—He is going to give you a river of pleasures, an abundance of them. Pleasure was invented and produced in heaven, overwhelming the spirit and soul of the believer.

Deep down inside we sometimes feel that if we follow God, we will somehow be cheated a bit. You have heard folks comment,

"Well, I want to sow my wild oats." If you knew the result of wild oats, you wouldn't want to sow them. If you do, you're going to penalize yourself. So many of us have bought Satan's lie that God is going to cheat us. The devil whispers, "God's going to mess up your life for sure. He's going to take all the fun out of your life. He's the original cosmic killjoy. He's plotting to make your life miserable. He wants to make you depressed and poor." Give Satan credit. He is a skillful liar (see John 8:44).

In the salvation of God there is full *satisfaction*. One of the best illustrations is found in John 2, at the wedding feast in Cana of Galilee where Jesus turned the water into wine. The governor of the feast tasted the miraculous wine and exclaimed, "Thou hast kept the good wine until now" (v. 10). In other words, "You have saved the best until last." That can only apply to God. Satan puts his best foot forward first. When the prodigal son left home with his inheritance and went to the "far country" to live as he chose, Satan gave the boy his best shot, but the kid ended up in the hog pen, starving to death. That's always how it is when one dances to the devil's music.

But not so with God. I shall never forget the day He came into my heart and saved me. I shall never forget the night when he touched my heart and called me to preach. It was an exciting time, and, oh, how precious and wonderful God has been over all these years. And God is more precious today than ever before. We used to sing "Every day with Jesus is sweeter than the day before." What He gives is better now than it has ever been. His grace gifts are superior and excellent right now, and they will be better tomorrow. God gives abundantly, but Satan cheats you, lies to you. He promises, "Follow Me, and I will give you this and that." Satan never gives you anything but misery. He always depletes you.

Yet, God gives, and His giving is filled with satisfaction. He will fill the longings and desires of your heart with His graceful presence. He provides a fountain of life, giving us spiritual eyes so we can see light—all of that speaks of joy and purity, truth and clarity. Life and light are two essentials of genuine spiritual experience. These are the opposite of darkness and death that envelop a person who follows Satan's way. What a "so great" salvation we have! The life that excels sees the *fulness of salvation*.

Finally, the life that excels sees:

III. The Faithfulness of the Savior

God is faithful. He will remain true to His Word. Verses 10-12 highlight two things the Lord will always do. First, He will *delight the saints*. "O continue thy lovingkindness unto them that know thee; and thy righteousness to the upright in heart" (v. 10). Note the prayer for God to "continue." He will never let us down. You can count on the Savior to be delivering delight and continuing His mercy and grace in your life.

You can also bank on Him to *denounce the sinner*. "Let not the foot of pride come against me, and let not the hand of the wicked remove me" (v. 11). He looked at those who had rebelled against God and had made wickedness their god, and he pointed the finger—there they are. Workers of iniquity were already fallen, cast down, and they would not be able to rise. Yet, the psalmist was still in the struggle and was still being opposed. This psalm is couched in the conflict between the wickedness of godless people and the godliness of the psalmist. Although under intense pressure from evil enemies, in God's eyes they were already cast down. They were already judged and would not be able to rise.

Through the eyes of faith, the psalmist knew that God was going to be faithful, even though it may have appeared for a time that evil had its ascendancy. But the truth is: the fate of the wicked and the doom of Satan are already signed, sealed, and delivered. Their death notice is already known. The Savior will be faithful. He would not be a faithful Savior if He allowed evil to triumph, if He allowed wickedness to succeed. The evil ones have "had it." In the end the saint will have the best of both worlds. He has the righteousness and the resources of God in this life, and then he has life for all of eternity—all because of the faithfulness of the Savior.

The whole essence of this psalm is another reminder that we can trust God. In fact, we *must* trust God. Don't allow a place for evil in your life. Don't listen to the whispers of wickedness or rebellion in your heart. Hallow that place for God in your life. Let Him speak to your spirit. Respond to Him. He will not shortchange you. You will be satisfied with the prosperity of His house, and He will make you to drink from rivers of pleasure. You will experience the fountain of life. You will have light in abundance.

The life that excels sees *the futility of sin, the fullness of salvation,* and *the faithfulness of the Savior*. You can rely on Him. Never will you go wrong obeying Him. For now and eternity you will bask in the life that excels!

4
Reaching Up From Despair

Psalm 42

The old song "Am I Blue?" could easily have been written by the psalmist. In Psalms 42 and 43—which were perhaps originally one psalm—the psalmist was "in the pits." You name it—he was depressed, disappointed, discouraged, down, stressed out. He was feeling "mighty low."

This psalm lays before us two aspects for every believer's life. On the one hand we are called to live in eternity with our minds and hearts set on God; on the other, we are also commanded to live in time with our minds and bodies under pressures that cannot and should not be ignored. How can we possibly do both? This psalm instructs us to take seriously both of these aspects in our lives. It is always tragic when a person seems to lie separated from the presence of God. It is sad when a person who once walked with God backslides and no longer senses His presence.

In the context of both psalms we view not only a heart hungering for God but also literally gasping for worship in the sanctuary. For whatever reason, the psalmist who wrote these words was separated from the presence of God's people. Sometimes illness, infirmity, or other circumstances will keep us from fellowship and worship. When a person drifts away from God, and God is not as precious to him as before, it is doubly sad. There is severe cause for alarm and concern when such is the situation. What happens many times—and we have all experienced it—is that suddenly we realize how thirsty we actually are, and how desperately we miss the presence of God. There is an emptiness and a dissatisfaction when we wander away from the Lord and no longer walk in companionship with and obedience to Him.

Psalm 42 is a portrait of an individual who was climbing from the depths to the heights. This is where most Americans are. Depression is epidemic. There are at least 2,000 suicides every day in the world. In the United States alone there are more than four million people who require special medical help for depression every year. And all of this is very relevant to our relationship with God. How does it work together?

Our enemy, Satan, wants to discourage us and will do all he can to make us despair. He throws his monkey wrench into our works. Having to live in a hostile world doesn't help, does it? Living and working around people who don't give a rip for God certainly is not easy. There are many factors that add to our depression; then many Christians add to their guilt by feeling they shouldn't be depressed! Even the greatest men of God were depressed at one time or another.

Believe me, depression is a normal part of our lives. Rain, for instance, is absolutely essential for health and life on this planet, but we wouldn't want rain all the time. Right? When there is too little rain, parching drought is the result. When there is too much rain, there is flooding, and we are overwhelmed with it. Yet, we need some rain. We can't have all sunshine. We also must have night. God set it up where we have daylight and darkness. So both darkness and daylight are necessary.

But the problem arises. There is a normal depression we will experience in the course of our lives, but it becomes abnormal when it lingers without abatement, and sometimes nothing we can do helps. Everything we try seems to make it worse. When it hangs on, then the depression gets out of hand. Most of us can readily identify with the psalmist in this matter, and we need to examine it. How does the Christian reach up from despair?

The Christian has supernatural resources the non-Christian does not have. When an unsaved individual comes to discouragement, despair, and depression, he may use drugs, alcohol, recreation, or sex as escape valves. But the unbeliever finds that when he tries to escape into these devices, ultimately he has not escaped *himself* and must face *himself*. In fact, his escapist tactics only become links in a chain that strengthens the imprisonment he has experienced. Escapism only forges another link in that chain. But the Christian does have resources he can call upon, and that is the gist of this psalm.

Now this is for sure at the outset. Making us feel guilty because we are discouraged or depressed is not the answer. It only drives us further into depression. Our emotions cannot change on command. If I tell you, "Don't feel depressed," that is an impossible command. The answer is not trying to feel bad because we feel bad; not becoming depressed because we are depressed. All of that compounds the problem.

There are times when our depression has physical causes and ought to have medical attention. For instance, certain forms of illness can cause depression. Erratic blood pressure, abnormal blood sugar, and other chemical imbalances can contribute to depression. When there is acute or severe depression, a competent Christian counselor ought to be enlisted. But there are steps all of us can take to overcome depression. Just as surely as night follows day, all of us have periods of discouragement. So depression and discouragement are a normal part of our lives, but they can become a wedge to drive us away from God, to separate us from those we love, and to destroy our lives.

There is practical, applicable help in this psalm. There are three things that I want to show you in this psalm. First of all, there is:

I. The Desire of the Psalmist

He writes in verses 1 through 4—

As the hart panteth after the water brooks, so panteth my soul after thee, O God: when shall I come and appear before God? My tears have been my meat day and night, while they continually say unto me, Where is thy God? When I remember these things, I pour out my soul in me: for I had gone with the multitude, I went with them to the house of God, with the voice of joy and praise, with a multitude that kept holyday.

His basic desire, first of all, was to have a heart for God. Within his heart there was a consuming passion to have spiritual intimacy with God, to feel Him, to sense His presence. I am convinced every individual has that same desire and longing. The person separated from the grace of God, who has not received eternal life, may not be aware there is an emptiness in his life only God can fill. Those of us who have been saved through the experience of conviction, repentance, and faith, know that what we really need is the Lord. The writer's desire was once again being able to worship in the house of the Lord, sensing close to his heart the presence of the Lord.

The question for us is—does God hear us? Does God really intervene in our lives? Can God honestly make a difference? Remember that Jesus invites: "if any man thirst, let him come unto me, and drink. He that believeth on me, as the scripture hath said, out of his belly shall flow rivers of living water" (John 7:37b-38). "O yes, He cares, I know He cares, His heart is touched with my grief." Absolutely.

Every person who hungers and thirsts after God's kingdom will gather the bounty of God's response. Billions have cried, thirsting for Him, and He has met their needs—and He will do it for us today. Also, the psalmist's desire was not only for the presence of God but also for the house of God. In verse 4 he remembered a vast procession winding its way to the house of God. There were jubilant songs of praise to God going to and in the house of worship. In Psalm 43 there is a similar situation: "Let them bring me unto thy holy hill, and to thy tabernacles. Then I will go unto the altar of God, . . . yea, upon the harp will I praise thee, O God my God" (vv. 3b-4). God intends for us to have a place where we worship together. The entire history of human relationship with God refers to sacred places where people commune with God. Sometimes it was in the isolation of a Jacob at Bethel, but it involved a sacred place. When you have a longing for God, you will also pine for His house.

Love for God that does not result in a corresponding love for His house is unnatural. God has commanded us to gather together. The born-again believer is inextricably joined to his spiritual brothers and sisters in the body of Christ. We are many members, but we are "all one" and we, the body, need to be united. In spite of the psalmist's discouragement, he had a burning desire for God and His place of worship.

We cannot minimize corporate worship. When we meet together we draw strength from one another. First there is a desire. This man recognized he had a deep desire for the things of God. Second, this psalm speaks about:

II. The Despair of the Psalmist

My tears have been my meat day and night, while they continually say unto me, Where is thy God? (v. 3).

Why art thou cast down, O my soul? and why art thou disquieted [disturbed] in me? hope thou in God: for I shall yet praise him for the help of his countenance. O my God, my soul is cast down within me (vv. 5-6a).

Deep calleth unto deep at the noise of thy waterspouts: all thy waves and thy billows are gone over me (v. 7).

I will say unto God my rock, Why hast thou forgotten me? why go I mourning because of the oppression of the enemy? As with a sword in my bones, mine enemies reproach me; while they say daily unto me, Where is thy God? Why art thou cast down, O my soul? and why are you disquieted within me? (vv. 9-11a).

A horrid picture of despair! This psalm gives us a clue to most of our depression. Oftentimes, depression is selfish, when we focus on ourselves too much, when we begin to dwell on *our* problems, *our* needs, *our* wants, *our* desires. In verse 4 the psalmist was upset because his plans were not fulfilled. He wanted to return to the house of God, and he couldn't. In verse 3 he was "bluer than blue." His feelings needed improving. He was in the midst of the people but apparently was extremely lonely. He seemed to cry all the time. He literally drank or ate his tears. "My tears have been my meat day and night." Throughout both Psalms 42 and 43, he wanted his questions answered, his plans fulfilled, and his feelings improved. In fact, in the sixteen verses of these psalms, the psalmist asks "why" ten times. In one instance he asked "when" once and "where" twice—thirteen questions. He merely wanted his questions answered.

He was so wrapped up in himself that he had trouble seeing God. If you want to stay depressed, major on yourself. Examine yourself, think of yourself more than others.

His emotions had become ingrown. "My tears have been my meat day and night, while they continually say to me, Where is thy God?" He was a grown man, but his tear ducts were overactive. How often our tears reflect the depression and the discouragement we feel. *Floods of tears.* Then he moaned about *floods of turmoil.* Verse 7 refers to the turmoil of a river flooding and monstrous rapids and cateracts boiling and churning. Here is a gripping picture of an overwhelming flood that inundates him: "all thy waves and thy billows are gone over me" (v. 7*b*). That phrase is almost the same as Jonah used (2:3) when he lamented, "All thy waves and thy billows passed over me." He next refers to *floods of trouble*. "Deep calleth unto deep" is as if he saw a wave rolling down the river with another right behind, with the one in front calling out to the one in back. Floods of trouble plagued him. Then there were *floods of testing*. In verses 9 and 10 his enemies reared their gross heads, asking, "Where is thy God?" He was tested at the point of his faith. The committed Christian faces this today. "Where is your God? Why does He allow you to suffer like this? Why doesn't He come to your rescue? Doesn't He care? Is He unable to do it? *Where is your God?*" All the psalmist could do was weep and suffer and long for a visitation from God.

The important thought about your depression is not *that* you get out of it but *what* you get out of it. What do you learn from it? If your heart genuinely desires God, then the experience that could tear you down will actually build you up! The darkness of depression eventually can become the most fruitful time of your life.

I heard that plants do not grow in the daytime but at night. They receive the supply of the sun and the atmosphere in the daytime, and at night they expand and grow. This is also true of individuals. Your most significant growth is not when all is rosy. We do not grow in the sunlight but rather in the darkness of life.

So, what can a Christian do amid despair? The victorious Christian life is not without struggle. The apostle Paul in Ephesians 6 reminded us we are in a spiritual warfare, a serious business. Many of God's greatest leaders have fought with depression, and God was able to use that depression. Martin Luther, the founder of the Reformation, was known to have deep fits of depression. Nothing would help, even when he was able to translate the Bible into German. Listen to his own words: "For more than a week I was close to the gates of death and hell. I trembled in all of my members. Christ was wholly lost. I was shaken by desperation and by blasphemy of God."

Does that sound to you like a hero of the faith? Depressed. Discouraged. Yet, Luther also confessed that depression was beneficial, for he said without those experiences no one can understand scriptural faith and the fear and love of God. In other words, if we never were depressed we would never realize God could help us with it. It can become a precious opportunity for us to discover God.

Charles Haddon Spurgeon, extolled as one of the greatest preachers of all time, was often in the "pits." In the latter years of his life he spent months at a time on the French Riviera to escape from the pressures that complicated his life, and most of the time he was physically and emotionally in despair. Spurgeon wrote a letter to his church after being gone several months. Part of it went: "The furnace still glows around me. Since I last preached to you I have been brought very low. My flesh has been tortured with pain and my spirit has been prostrate with depression. With some difficulty I write these lines in my bed, mingling them with the groans of pain and the songs of hope. I am as a potter's vessel when it is utterly broken, useless and laid aside. Nights of watching and days of weeping have been mine, but I hope the cloud is passing. There are dungeons," he wrote, "beneath the castle of despair." He often found himself in those dungeons.

John the Baptist became dreadfully depressed. He certainly had valid reasons. John was in prison and eventually was beheaded for his preaching. He was "the second Elijah," the "forerunner" to the Messiah, who had, upon seeing Jesus, authoritatively announced, "Behold the Lamb of God, which taketh away the sin of the world (John 1:29). He who had preached Jesus began to doubt Jesus. In Matthew 11:2-3 we find, "Now when John had heard in the prison the works of Christ, he sent two of his disciples, And said unto him, Art thou he who should come, or do we look for another?" Can you imagine that? The man who had preached with an exclamation point now queried with a question mark.

He was down in that moment, but Jesus did not reprimand him. In fact, it is amazing that on the day when John the Baptist said the worst thing he had ever said about Jesus, Jesus said the best thing He ever said about John the Baptist! Jesus praised John with: "Among them that are born of women there hath not risen a greater than John the Baptist" (v. 11*a*). When the prophet was caught in the trap of discouragement and despair, Jesus added the most unfamiliar Beatitude in the Bible. In fact, if I asked you to list all of the Beatitudes you would never think of this one. "Blessed is he, whosoever shall not be offended in me" (v. 6). Here is a twentieth-century translation of that. "Blessed is he who does not become upset by how I run my business." The Lord is running His business on schedule, carrying out His program according to His plans and His specification. God does not operate on our timetable, and sometimes it does not add up in our computers. But God is still in control, and we need to realize we can trust Him. We cannot always *trace* God, but we can always *trust* Him.

Many Christians themselves are in the dungeon of despair. It may be illness or bereavement. It may be your heart lies in the grave. It may be financial; it may be relationships. "Iron bars do not a prison make," and we find ourselves in the cage of despair.

I do not understand everything God does or why He does it, but I refuse to be upset with how He does it. I refuse to find in Him a stumbling block. Isaiah 8:14 states that you will either perceive in God a sanctuary or a snare, a stumbling block or a snare on the one side but sustenance on the other side. God will either be to you a problem or a profit. If you try to explain God's strategies with your logic, and you demand that God satisfy your reason, then God is going to be a snare to you. I choose to locate in Him a sanctuary.

The psalmist was extremely depressed. Great people of God over the years have faced the same kind of experience. It is not wrong to be depressed. Read of Jesus' emotions in the garden of Gethsemane, and you will discover discouragement and depression. "My soul is exceedingly sorrowful, even unto death" (Matt. 26:38). He cried. It's what you do with depression, how you handle it, how you act and react in the midst of it.

We have first the psalmist's desire—his basic need. Then he painted a picture of despair. But then he spoke of:

III. The Delight of the Psalmist

"Hope thou in God: for I will yet praise him for the help of his countenance" (v. 5b). Now drink in verse 8. "Yet the Lord will command his lovingkindness in the daytime, and in the night his song shall be with me, and my prayer unto the God of my life."

And in verse 11 he sings, "Hope thou in God: for I shall yet praise him, who is the health of my countenance, and my God.

The psalmist was willing to rest his case with God, to lay it at His feet. Those troubles only led him to God. Do your troubles, discouragement, and depression lead you to God? Do they cause you to fall on your knees and come to God? In the dark hour He is able to reveal His best to you and to me. We are to delight in God. Our faith and hope are undergirded with strong convictions. In verse 6 he wrote—"I remember thee from the land of Jordan." He recalled when he went into the house of God. He reminisced about what God had done in his life in the past. If you look into the past and merely see yourself, then you will begin to contrast circumstances, and your depression will worsen. But if you look in the past and remember what God has done for and in you, then God will use that to help you delight in Him.

The answer to depression is hope, and our hope is not in ourselves but in God. He speaks of delighting not only in the *hope* of God but also in the *help* of God. Each time the psalmist mentioned hope, he also spoke of the Lord's help. "For I shall yet praise him for the help of his countenance" (v. 5*b*). In verse 11 he spoke of God "as the health of my countenance." The thought here is that God's face is never marked with disappointment. God is never discouraged.

The psalmist frankly laid the issue before the Lord Himself. The moment he admitted that he had an unfulfilled desire, he began to delight in the Lord, and was on the way to recovery. God's song would be with him, and his prayer would be unto God in the night (v. 8). If you wait for the daylight it may never come. In the dungeon of depression, in the night, may God's song be in your heart, and may your prayer be unto Him.

How will you face your depression? Endure it? Escape it? Or learn from it? William Cowper wrote numerous poems and hymn lyrics. Many folks do not understand that William Cowper was constantly besieged by depression, and many times even endeavored to commit suicide. Yet, Cowper wrote these words:

> God moves in a mysterious way His wonders to perform;
> He plants His footsteps in the sea, And rides upon
> the storm.

Deep in unfathomable mind Of never failing skill
He treasures up His bright designs, And works His
   sovereign will.

Ye fearful saints, fresh courage take:
The clouds you so much dread
Are big with mercy, and shall break in blessings
   on your head.

Judge not the Lord by feeble sense, But trust Him
   for His grace;
Behind a frowning providence He hides a smiling
   face.

His purpose will ripen fast, unfolding every hour.
The bud may have a bitter taste, But sweet
   will be the flower.

Blind unbelief is sure to err And scan His work in
   vain;
God is His own interpreter, And He will make it plain.

Despair. He knew it, but he also knew that in the midst of the
night, God was there.

What is your desire? Is it for God? Whether you know it or not, it
is. Whether you admit it or not, the longing, the frustration, the
emptiness, the searching of your heart is for God. Despair may
overwhelm you. Troubles and trials may overwhelm you, but if you
will delight yourself in the Lord in the night, God will bless you in
the midst of the experiences when Satan intends to tear you down.

The bottom line is: The cure for depression is clinging to Jesus,
not in all of our schemes and all of our strength, but in thirsty and
panting desire to have Jesus supreme in our hearts!

5
Depresssed or Delighted?

Psalm 43

A distinct difference exists between the Psalms and the rest of the Bible. In other parts of the Bible it is "thus saith the Lord," but the Psalms portray man in his dilemmas as he cries out to God. God responds to the personal needs of common folks like you and me. Bear in mind that Psalms 42 and 43 are companions.

We are not sure who wrote Psalms 42 and 43, though many believe they were written by King Hezekiah as he was under the threat and intimidation of vicious Assyria. In these two psalms there is a pendulum swing of emotions. The writer bounces off the walls of depression and delight, going from one extreme to the other. He inherited the Assyrian menace from his father, King Ahaz, and now he was preparing to do battle or to negotiate with that enemy to the north. His emotions were swinging, and he was submerged in doubt. He was praising, yet he was depressed and delighted. Have you ever done that? Sure you have. You have felt manic-depressive. All of us have at least hit the depression wall. We can identify with the writer because that's where we live. Those blue emotions are common to all of us. Depression.

I understand there are sometimes physical reasons for depression, even a tumor or a chemical imbalance that causes and creates depression. We owe our thanks to skilled physicians who can help us by ministering to our physical needs at such a down time. But most of the time (and I want to deal with most of the time), depression is self-induced. We do it to ourselves. We actually choose to be depressed. In fact, you can decide which you're going to be—*depressed* or *delighted*. Many times it is your choice. You can't say "the devil made me do it," because he can't make you do anything. Delighted or depressed, we have all have had that kind of experience.

Depression is a drastic problem around the world. It is estimated there are over 2,000 suicides a day worldwide. At least four million Americans last year had such serious depression that they required medical attention. Multiplied thousands of others underwent various methods of counseling. But, without apology and with excitement, I declare that the Christian has resources not available to the non-Christian. We have carte blanche to tremendous help which is not accessible to those outside of Christ.

Psalms 42 and 43 give the first clue to the self-inducement of depression. In fact, there are fifty-one personal pronouns in these two psalms. The pronoun "I" is mentioned fourteen times; "me," sixteen times; "my," twenty-one times. On the other side, God is referred to only twenty times and "the Lord," only once. The psalmist has an unhealthy fixation upon himself, his ego. *Me, my,* and *mine.* That is one reason why there is such widespread discouragement and despair.

It is dangerous to look too much at yourself. It can plunge you into "I" trouble. If we look at ourselves long enough, it can lead to depression. Now, you can go through life like that. With God's support I prefer to think I'm working hard at disciplining myself to accomplish His purposes. I frankly don't want to look too close because then I'll focus on *myself,* on *my* problems, *my* inconsistencies, *my* weaknesses, and soon enough I'll be depressed. It is detrimental to look too long at yourself. If you see yourself everywhere you turn, you are in trouble. If everything you see reminds you of *your* problems, *your* difficulties, *your* needs, depression will be your constant companion.

This explains why changing circumstances doesn't cure depression. Suppose you move to another area. It doesn't solve your depression because *you* go with *you* when you go. You will carry the same attitude, the same self-fixation, and the same self-centeredness. You will likely pack up the difficulties you were supposed to leave behind. Depression is often the normal result of being too caught up in ourselves.

The psalmist was at that juncture. He had a human justification to drive him to insanity. He was suffering from the propaganda of Assyria, an ungodly nation. There was enough truth in their character assassination that it created real problems within his nation and in his own mind. At that time the Assyrian army was menacingly awesome. This psalm is about the psalmist's realization that his only strength was in God. His joy and strength lay in God, but he boomeranged from despair and depression and back to delight again.

Praise the Lord, he ended up on the delight side. In this psalm are the struggles of a man climbing from the depths to the heights—from despair and depression to delight, joy, hope, and praise.

In the first two verses there is:

I. A Distressed Cry

"Judge me, O God," he prays. "Plead my cause against an ungodly nation: O deliver me from the deceitful and unjust man. For thou are the God of my strength: Why doest thou cast me off? why go I mourning because of the oppression of the enemy?" (43:1-2)

First, there is his complaint. It was, in essence, "I'm being oppressed, ridiculed, attacked, misrepresented. Our enemy is gathering on our northern border, and they are stronger than we are. Lord, plead my cause. Judge me, O God." In this unusual cry, he first complains about his situation, but then he begs, "God, I want You to judge me." This is unique because most people plead the mercy of God. He pleads for the justice of God. His heart was right with God and, more than all else, he longed for a great spiritual awakening in his nation. Because of his contact with God he did not ask for God to view him with mercy but rather pleaded, "God, justify me. Vindicate me. Plead my cause. Judge me"—a daring request.

Most of us fear the judgment of God and would seldom ask for judgment and justice. Just as we don't want to look too closely at our own lives because we become depressed, neither do we want God looking too close! His was a tremendous thought. If you study biblical history you will discover that Hezekiah was referred to as "good King Hezekiah." He had instigated religious reforms and had called the people away from idol worship. The people could have cared less. They had undercut the reforms of Hezekiah with restless discontent and bitter grumbling. No wonder he was discouraged and doubtful. In verse 2, he was asking, "God, don't look at anybody else. Look at me. There's no place else for me to go but to You. Why do you cast me off?" He was grasping and groping.

"Judge me" led him to communion and worship as he prayed in verse 3: "O send out thy light and thy truth: let them lead me; let them bring me unto thy holy hill, and to thy tabernacles." He has retraced his steps to Psalm 42, where there was emphasis toward public worship of the congregation. He was wanting to lead his nation in sacrifice and song, in worship and praise. It is an unparalleled blessing to any people when its leaders lead them toward God. That is why we are called upon to pray for our leaders at all levels. The king's most intense desire was that the communion in his heart would ultimately express itself in coming to the place of worship to offer God his sacrifice, his song of praise, and his recommitment to the Lord.

Worship for the believer is more essential than blood and breath—private *and* public. Many people have alibied, "I don't have to go to church to worship." No, you don't. But you probably won't worship if you don't. You don't need public worship? Then you're smarter than God. Quit kidding yourself. If you want God to bless your life as He really wants to, you need the communion and worship experience with God's people.

We need one another. None of us are superstars or supersaints. We must draw strength from one another. Strength and sustenance are imparted when we lift our voices praising the Lord and when we gather around the Word of God. That allows God's Holy Spirit especially to touch us. The psalmist was communing with God privately and in the place of public worship. Here was a *distressed cry*.

Then there is:

II. A Distinct Consolation

"Then will I go unto the altar of God, unto God my exceeding joy: yea, upon the harp will I praise thee, O God, my God" (v. 4). First we see his exaltation, exploding in his adoration as he sings about God being his "exceeding joy" and then the *exaltation* as his personal joy becomes the object and subject of his praise. Extolling God's praises, the psalmist exults, "O God, my God." His joy was

God. "Unto God my exceeding joy." That literally means "God, the gladness of my joy."

What gives you joy? If your happiness is found in your circumstances—in your relationships, your feelings, and your successes as you would measure them—you are going to remain depressed most of the time because circumstances are incapable of giving you joy. All the so-called joys stemming from mere human relationships, friendships, employee/employer ties, and challenges are not capable of satisfying the hunger of your heart. Outside of the Lord, you will have depression as a constant companion.

The reason the psalmist could be resilient is because God was the gladness of his joy. He rejoiced in the presence of God, the Word of God, the truth of God, and the will of God. God was the wellspring of his joy. He delighted in the Lord and sought Him with all of his heart. The Word of God, clearly from beginning to end, elaborates about that kind of concentration on the things of God. We occasionally taste a spiritual morsel here and there, and we don't find satisfaction. Why? Because God was never meant to be something—He was meant to be *everything*. He was never meant to be a joy in life. He was meant to be *the* joy in life. He was not meant to be an addendum to life—He was meant to be *life*. So the psalmist, amid his desperate circumstances, testified, "I exalt God as my joy." When your world seems to cave in, God is still there. All else may go wrong, but you still have His presence in Christ. The *exaltation* of God. Then the *exultation* of God. "[Though art] my exceeding joy: yea, upon the harp will I praise thee, O God."

His intellect told him there was nothing to be rejoicing about, but his heart told him he had everything about which to rejoice. He was delighted in that God was his joy and strength. We may as well learn that if we wait until we are intellectually satisfied, hoping to seize joy, we never will find it. Have you ever tried mountain climbing? Our family used to visit Southern Colorado every summer to hike. I'd remark, "Hey, when we just get to the crest of that hill we'll be at the top of the mountain." I was kidding myself. It finally seemed that there was no end to those mountains. No matter how often and how long we climbed, there was always another hill, another mountain.

Life is like that. There's always going to be another hill, another barrier, another adverse problem. Vocationally, emotionally, and socially, there will always be another hill to climb. If you're waiting until your mind has all circumstances like you want them to be, you'll never rejoice. You'll never be delighted. Underline it. Praise and exalt the Lord. Even when your head doesn't give you a reason to rejoice, your heart will rejoice because the Lord is there.

Finally, in this last verse, there is:

III. A Dramatic Confidence

First, there is a *challenge.* "Why art thou cast down, O my soul? and why art thou disquieted within me?" The challenge is toward God. Why? In fact, ten times in these two psalms the question "why" is asked. It is not wrong to question God. Rather, it is wrong to accuse God. I must be absolutely fair and honest with you—God may not answer all of your questions.

The Book of Job grappled with the question, "Why do good people suffer?" Read the whole Book of Job, but God never answers the question. When the Book ended, though, Job had forgotten the question because he had a new vision of God. In Psalms 42 and 43 God never answers any of these thirteen questions as far as I can tell. Suppose God did answer all our questions? I am not sure. First of all, it wouldn't help because we couldn't understand it even if we knew the explanation. God's thoughts are higher than our thoughts. Second, though, even if we understood it, it couldn't help, because we do not rejoice due to explanations but because of the promises and presence of God.

When you allow God priority in your life, and let His Word have maximum exposure, being obedient to His design for you, you will experience profound joy, not because of explanations but because of God's presence and promises in your life. The psalmist actually challenges God. Hezekiah was simply being honest with God. God wants that from all of us. What's your problem? Trot it out. Stare it in the face. What is it? Undergoing financial straits? Confess it. Smarting because of a broken relationship? Lay it out. Going through physical need? Whatever is bothering you, stand it right in front of you and ask God about it.

Yes, challenge Him with it. That was Hezekiah's modus operandi. God doesn't want you to say, "Lord, everything's great," if it's not. He knows you better than that. Be honest with Him. You can't get by with lying to Him, anyway!

Remember that man who besought Jesus to heal his son "which hath a dumb spirit"? Jesus inquired, "If thou canst believe, all things are possible to him that believeth" (Mark 9:23). Do you recall the man's answer? "Lord, I believe; help thou mine unbelief?" (v. 24*b*). What a pitiful answer that was, but then Jesus healed his son. Why? The man had certain doubts, but he stared them in the face and said, "Lord, I believe, but I've got some doubts." Jesus replied, "That's good enough for me." The man dealt with his misgivings. Don't push your problem aside. Don't pretend it's not there. Are you rebellious? Are you resentful? Are you bitter? Are you apathetic? The greatest danger most people encounter is that they just don't care and don't care that they don't care!

Our society is so sophisticated and affluent that nothing particularly seems to bother us. We don't assault God—we just ignore Him. Is that your problem? Face it as Hezekiah did. In essence, he asked, "God, why do I do as I do? Why do I doubt?" He faced his problem honestly. There was the *challenge*, and when he came through the challenge, he caught *certainty*. Hope in God. "For I shall yet praise him, who is the health of my countenance, and my God."

The answer to depression is hope. We despair when we feel there is no hope. We are depressed when we sense that all hope is gone. Our only hope is in God. Our hope is not in our strength or our creativity—not in what we can do, what we think, what we are, what we have. Our hope is in God. Hope, not in ourselves, but in God. That hope guarantees future security. I have no idea what may come my way, but I know where I'm headed. Jesus holds my hand. He is not going to let any testing or temptation come my way but that there is victory available.

With each testing and temptation He is going to give me a way of escape that I may be able to bear it (see 1 Cor. 10:13). With my hand in His, my hope in Him, my anticipation of His presence, my reliance on the power of the Holy Spirit, and my anticipation of His coming again in the Person of His Son, I have hope that the future is secure in Christ. I have a certainty that banishes depression and escorts me to delight and hope in Him.

Every time the psalmist mentions "hope" in these two psalms, he says either "the help of his countenance" (42:5) or "the health of my countenance" (42:11; 43:5). Those phrases mean that your hope, or lack of it, shows in your countenance. Your face reveals that hope. This truth teaches me that God is not sad. God's face is not distressed, not depressed. If God is the health of my countenance, then that indicates He is good for my outward attitude because of my inward hope. God is helpful for my countenance. You've heard this expression, "If you're happy, then tell your face." Express it. What you are is often written all over your face. When our hope is anchored in God, there is certainty in our lives. There is healthfulness.

The struggle is common to all of us. The answer to our struggles is hope in God. We "cultured" Americans think, *The answer to my financial problems is a million dollars.* No, it's not. You'd probably misuse that just as you have done before. "The answer to my problems is I just need to be healthy again." You didn't take care of your health when you had it. What makes you think you would if you had it back?

Paul testified, "When I am weak, then I am strong (2 Cor. 12:10). The gist of his discovery was: "I will glory in my weakness because when I'm weak, I'm strong in Christ." He wasn't delighted and excited that he was weak and struggling, but he recognized that his weakness and struggle ushered the strength of God into his life. Anything that brings us to God is good.

A student of nature once was watching a moth as it struggled to emerge slowly from its chrysalis stage. Day after day that moth tried to emerge from the very tiny hole in the end of its cocoon. This student was concerned for the moth, so with his penknife he enlarged the hole a little bit to make it easier for the chrysalis to break free and become a moth. The next day that happened. The chrysalis had become a moth, but its wings were imperfect. It could flutter, but it couldn't fly. And when night fell, it was dead.

That unnatural assistance had robbed the moth of the strength from the struggle, and he didn't have the power to win in life because he hadn't endured the full struggle to arrive. It is vital for you and me to remember that the struggle is part and parcel of our lives. Bouncing off the walls of depression and back to delight is going to happen because we struggle. Struggle is a necessary daily ingredient for our lives. You wouldn't be stronger if you never had a struggle. You would be weaker if you never had a problem. The fact is, you'd be pitifully weaker than you are now.

History unveils dramatic evidence of that. The greatest ancient civilizations did not begin along the fertile deltas of the Nile or the Tigris and Euphrates Rivers. Rather, perhaps the most aggressive of all was found on the barren plains of Attica among the Greeks. Lacking the resources that led to wealth and luxury, the Greeks had to rely on the struggles of difficult existence and their own creativity. Thus, from Greece emerged perhaps the greatest philosophers of the world. From Greece came forth the greatest art and sculptures of the world. From Greece blossomed forth the greatest builders and architects of the world. It happened because the Greeks did not have a favored existence but rather had to struggle. And, of course, the precious language of the New Testament was *koine* Greek.

Struggle is basic in our nation. If you read the true history of America, you will see words like *courage, conquest, struggle, determination,* and *hardship*. Those are the apropos words which describe the beginning of this nation, and struggle is why this has been a mighty nation. Thank God for the struggle! Don't try to avoid it. The psalmist did struggle. He was misrepresented and slandered. He had a potential enemy about to descend on him in destruction, but he didn't pray for the struggle to be over. But, rather than focusing on himself, which always brings depression—he gazed on God who always delivers delight.

Depressed or delighted? It is your choice.

6

Discovering Oases in the Desert

Psalm 63

David was in a barren, desolate desert. He was literally running for his life. We are not exactly sure who was pursuing him. Perhaps it was in David's earlier years when King Saul was trying to snuff him out. The young singer-shepherd had risen to prominence, and King Saul, in his green-eyed jealousy and envy, was plotting against him.

The second possibility is that he was fleeing from his own seditious son, Absalom. You will recall that Absalom returned to Jerusalem, instigated a coup d'etat in the government—a rebellion, a revolution—and led the very people who had cheered David as the king to rebel against him. There he was in the wilderness, perhaps fleeing from his own son and betrayed by his own subjects. He was stripped of physical and human resources that could make him significant and important. He was bereft.

When we are in a situation where everything we depend on from a human standpoint is snatched away, we have only one place to go—and that's inside. David understood that he could go on without the outward physical trappings that had adorned his life, but he could not make it if he was empty inside. So, in the quiet and solitude of the desert, he sought the face of God. He had stopped running and ceased fighting. His panic had subsided, and he had entered into a quiet place to call for God's presence.

This psalm delineates how David refreshed himself and recaptured his excitement, his enthusiasm, and his fervor for the concerns of God. The desert became his special place as he turned to God. This psalm relates how David discovered streams in the desert, how he drew forth refreshing water for his dry, parched soul. All of us need a special place where we can draw aside, close out the world, and feed upon the resources of God for our lives. let me make that personal for us.

(Here follows a personal challenge to the author's former church, First Baptist Church of Euless, Texas.)

I carry you to a desert that is one of the greatest churches in America. It has one of the outstanding opportunities facing any church anywhere. It is filled with tremendous people—those who are willing to sacrifice, to persevere, to share, to witness, to love, to care—but a people who are mentally and spiritually fatigued in the desert, if you please.

We've been drained these last several years. Denominational discord and controversy has clamored for our attention. And though we've not sought it, we've found ourselves embroiled in it. Political voices have cried for our affection across the land. Theological error has knocked at our door. Moral and ethical issues continue to call out for redress. In fact, this year we will spend much of our time fighting the evil of organized gambling and the potential for legalizing such in Texas. Many matters have devoured our time. And as pastor and as people, I'm afraid many times we have supported the good and missed the best in our lives.

Spiritual fatigue is real. We're tired. I'm tired. There's a weariness of spirit and soul. In the midst of all this, somehow we have found ourselves in the desert. Many of us have lost our spiritual fervor, our excitement, our compassion. You can remember a time when you came with expectancy to this auditorium realizing that God was going to move supernaturally. Now many of us arrive, sitting with hollow eyes and empty hearts in a wilderness of weariness. Oh, it wasn't our intention to be in the desert. It never is, but we found ourselves going more for God and spending less time with Him in the process. All output and no input make a desert—pouring out our energy to *do things, to accomplish things.* That is one of the reasons why I have accepted only a handful of speaking engagements. For about ten years I have gone at least once or twice a week all over this country until I have found myself so dry, so empty, saying the words but weary in my spirit out in a desert. We are doing more and enjoying it less. That may well describe us all.

Look around and you notice the dropouts. This is very real

because some of you are going to become dropouts if you don't deal with what I'm talking about today. I look across this congregation and I see empty places where several years ago there were vibrant people who are now gone. Most of them didn't go to another church—they merely dropped out. They became fatigued. Nothing is more wearying, nothing is more fatiguing, nothing is more tiresome than trying to do the work of God in the energy of the flesh! In those circumstances you will always find yourself in a desert.

How do we restore that spiritual passion? How do we recapture the ecstasy, the excitement? How do we do the right things with the right relationship? When we begin to retreat to the desert, we have plenty of contacts but few relationships. We do a lot, but we miss the fervent spirit in which we ought to be moving.

Psalm 63 deals with precisely this problem. It is a psalm about a man whose spirit was crushed. He was in the barren desert. Disloyalty had robbed him of his family and his supporters. The applause and the acclaim of the nation had turned against him. Fearful for his life, he cried out, "My soul thirsts for God. My flesh longs for You in a dry and thirsty land where no water is." Can you identify with that? Thirsting and longing—not simply for the mechanics of worship, but pining for something more. Your desert may be a modern office, a luxurious home, a secure joy, even fellowship in the church. But how do you escape the desert? How do you leave the weariness and tiredness of heart, soul, and mind that often occur in the ministry of the church? That's what this psalm is about.

If I have ever preached an autobiographical sermon, this is it. Maybe you can identify with it. How do you override the complacency of middle age? How do you overcome the contempt that familiarity breeds? How do you maintain spiritual intensity and excitement that is born out of a relationship with God? When the apostle Paul reached the end of his life he testified that he forgot the past things and he pressed on. (Phil. 3:13-14) And the words "press on" are a sports term. They speak of an athlete who is pouring every bit of energy and strength into reaching a goal. How do you do that? How do you come down to the end still pressing on to victory?

In this psalm David talked about four places. Gordon MacDonald devotes an entire book to this theme of restoring your spiritual passion. In this psalm David sang about four kinds of places necessary if you are to encounter streams in the desert.

If you are going to discover streams in the desert you need:

I. A Sacred Place

Look at verses 2 and 3. He says—"To see thy power and thy glory, so as I have seen thee in the sanctuary. Because thy loving-kindness is better than life, my lips shall praise thee." The first five verses treat the sacred place in David's life. There were no buildings or temples in the desert, but he remembered the sanctuary, the precious place of worship set apart for him to worship God. The emphasis in the sacred place was on the majesty, power, glory, and love of God. It is there that you remove your eyes from human vexations that occupy your time and you set your heart on God. You do not exit the desert doing things for God; you vacate the desert by setting your heart on God in a sacred place.

In his mind and heart once again, David visited the sanctuary. He had been overwhelmed by human power greater than his own. What do you do when an adversary is stronger than you? What do you do when you are defeated and frustrated? Suppose someone else lands the job you wanted? In the sacred place you turn your eyes upon God, and there His majesty and glory are the key.

Man has always had a sacred place. People claim they can worship without going to a church building. That's true, but they won't. The sacred place is untainted by distraction. How sorely we need a sacred place. We in America do not understand what it means to have a sacred place. We do not particularly reverence the sanctuary. What you will notice when you visit South Korea is that every individual who enters the sanctuary will sit down, bow his head, and pray before looking around. If one enters in the middle of your sermon, he bows his head and prays. In most of the churches as the music men and the ministers come to the platform they remove their shoes, and those on the platform will kneel by their chairs and pray.

To us in America nothing seems sacred. We're an all-sufficient, arrogant, self-righteous people. We have lost track of a sacred place set apart for us to somehow touch God. There is fatigue associated with intimidation and defeat, a weariness with being drained by people who seek to dominate our lives. Fatigue is often a concomitant of warfare, especially when we often wage war in our own strength. David was literally worn out. Isolation and terrible loneliness feed fatigue. And sooner or later, every one of us will feel betrayal, loneliness, and isolation. We must locate the sacred place where we can focus our attention on God. "To see thy power and thy glory, so as I have seen thee in the sanctuary" (v. 2). In verse 3 he writes of "thy loving-kindness." We could translate that "thy steadfast love."

There is a second kind of place he mentioned, and that is:

II. A Secluded, Secret Place

Notice in verses 6 and 7: "When I remember thee upon my bed, and meditate on thee in the night watches. Because thou hast been my help, therefore in the shadow of thy wings will I rejoice." The *secret place*. The *secluded place*. Most of us are leery of that place. We want people around us with busyness and activity. To be isolated alone with God is somehow a frightening prospect to many of us. But David declared that we need a secluded place. When he had insomnia—or when he chose not to sleep—in that secluded, secret place he meditated upon God.

Many of us use that secret place to refuel our bitterness, as a place to erect our defenses so we can protect ourselves and strategize our anger and retaliation. But not David. It was a place of renewal. There he reflected upon the times God had helped him. When he stood against Goliath he heard God promise, "I will be your help." When he fought the lion and the bear he heard God console him, "I will be your help." As he lay on his bed in the dark seasons he heard the Lord whisper as He did to Joshua: "I will be with you. I will not fail you or forsake you."

A third kind of place he mentions is:

III. A Safe Place

A safe place.—Notice he prays. ". . . Therefore in the shadow of thy wings will I rejoice (v. 7). As David thought about a safe place of protection where he could experience a fresh relationship with

God, he thought about the wings of a bird. We will often see birds in the desert, riding on the currents of the air, spiraling, circling, plunging, hovering. To restore his spiritual passion, he considered the wings of a bird. "In the shadow of thy wings will I rejoice." Wings are often symbols of God.

There are several basic facts that stand out in biblical references to the wings of God. One is warmth. Of course, overall is protection. Reflect on Jesus' words: "How often would I have gathered thy children together, even as a hen gathereth her chickens under her wings" (Matt. 23:37). Why does she gather them under her wings? For warmth, for protection. Wings refer to warmth and refuge. We all need a safe place of protection, trust, and refuge—a place where we can rejoice. Upon the wings of the wind the birds are free to soar, and to sing, and we're free under the wings of God to sing in our hearts and souls.

Then he refers to:

IV. A Secure Place

He continues, "My soul followeth hard after thee: thy right hand upholdeth me" (v. 8). The only secure place in an insecure world is in the hand of God. In Him there is confidence. Now remember the context of this psalm. David had experienced a humiliating defeat. His self-esteem had taken a dive, but he declared, "Thy right hand upholds [secures] me." The hand of God, particularly the right hand, is found repeatedly in Scripture. This expression has many basic connotations. It speaks of *safety; conviction*, for under the hand of God we find awareness of our need and sin; *sustenance; judgment; strength; disclosure*, for under the hand of God we learn and hear the will of God; *possession*, because we belong to God; *goodness; creation; works* and *deliverance* of God.

Confidence

Confidence is not a psychological attitude we work up on the basis of our self-assurance, not a reaction based on unrealistic hopes, but a sense of a power beyond ourselves. It is the sense of God's supernatural presence in our lives, holding us. Somehow in the desert place David found himself secure in the hands of God Himself, offering him tremendous inner strength and direction.

We have mastered the art of outward appearances. We are award-winning actors. To quote the old song, "I'm laughing on the outside, crying on the inside." We look content, even though we are dying by degrees. And Satan works overtime on that. The devil will tell you, "Look at that guy. You don't feel as he feels." Yet you don't really know how he feels. He may have mastered the art of pretending to feel a way he doesn't actually feel. Many could sing, "They call me the great pretender." From childhood we have been taught techniques to protect ourselves and to conceal our insecurities. "Big boys don't cry." And so many don't cry—except inside. And we mask our insecurity and hurt. Oh, we pretend perhaps by speaking confidently, laughing heartily, or taking risks.

When I was a kid we played "double dog dare you." "Boy, I'll do it because you dare me." It is all a part of the mask.

David was in the desert. The king. The spiritual and political leader of the nation. But he confessed, "The only place I found security was in the strong hand of God."

You and I need to stop frequently in the rat race of American life, amid bone-tiring, mind-dissolving days, and locate a secure place. We must somehow slip our spirit into the hand of God who promised Isaiah, "I will uphold you with my [victorious] right hand" (Isa. 41:10, NIV). Stop playing the game. It's not important that you impress me or others that you are "with it" or have "it under control." When you find yourself in the desert, it might be the very best place for you to be. Through the desolation and dearth of the desert he reached out and rediscovered God. Elijah, threatened by Jezebel, was wiped out even after his smashing victory on Mount Carmel where he had opposed 450 prophets of Baal. He fled to the desert wanting to die, but that desert became a sacred place where he found renewal and restoration.

For Simon Peter, his desert was the shoreline of the Sea of Galilee. He had betrayed his Savior in a brazen denial, but Jesus appeared on that shore, cooked him breakfast, and restored him, giving him a second chance. Jesus found Himself in the desert of Gethsemane. Some may think He was playing charades, but His testing was a life-and-death struggle. In that desert His flesh cried out, "I don't want to die. I don't want to go to the cross and endure the shame." Yet, His desert was a garden, but in that desert He resolved, "Not my will, but thine, be done" (Luke 22:42). The ultimate victory of Calvary was won in the desert.

Are you in a desert today? Do you hear yourself inside protesting, "I don't want to go through the dryness of another day. I can't stand these feelings, this isolation, this sense of desertion."

In the desert find a sacred, secluded, safe, and secure place where you can come upon an oasis in the desert—restoration of your spiritual passion.

7
Surviving the Mid-life Crisis

Psalm 71

All of us can identify with Psalm 71. It was written by a man who wanted to end up well. He wanted to reach the end of his life on a positive note, with a happy, fulfilled, and satisfied spirit. In addition, he wanted to be useful and to bask in the peace of God throughout his life.

This is a psalm that deals with a man who was wrestling, maybe for the first time, but specifically with his own mortality. He was facing the glaring truth that he would soon be passing into old age, and he understood that the passing years and the maturity process usher in special dangers and demands, even on the believer. Christians are not exempt from growing old or from the problems that accompany age. The psalmist understood that mature years not only create problems, but reveal problems— problems we push down and set aside, and they sometimes rear their ugly heads in these maturing years.

The psalmist had been blessed with a godly childhood. Yet, he took nothing for granted. He was aging, and he had seen exceptional trouble. In verse 7, he exclaimed: "I am as a wonder unto many." The Hebrew language reveals that he was virtually a spectacle because of all of his pressures, problems, and trials. Sadly, his troubles showed no signs of ceasing. He was going through the mid-life crisis, looking toward old age.

You might argue, "I'm too young for that." Really? Psychologists tell us the mid-life crisis period is thirty-five to fifty-five. For some it starts earlier than that.

A young lady was wringing her hands because she was about to be thirty years old. Terrible, isn't it? Growing old. Going into the middle-life years. There are tremendous changes occurring in our lives as we age, and we need to understand them, and how we can experience the power of God in spite of age. Some have called these middle years, "middlescent malaise." We know what adolescence is, but I speak of "middlescence" now—going through these passages of time—and when most people reach this period, they feel unhappy and withdrawn. They often lose their self-confidence; they can become uneasy; some retreat into hypochondria; others simply change their external circumstances. At this period, unfortunately many will change their marriages, their jobs, their professions. They will resume interrupted careers or maybe return to school. Many are the emotions with which we wrestle during mid life.

The key to it is that we become painfully aware of our mortality. When we were young we seldom thought about it. Then, I just couldn't imagine the world without me! I thought I would live on this earth forever. In mid-life, you face the stark reality that even you are going to age—and, yes, you are going to experience physical death, if the Lord tarries. You realize you are losing the touch of youth, the universal "currency" of Western civilization. We have put a premium on youth, its strength, agility, and resilience.

Our bodies begin to thicken, usually around the middle. My tapered shirts are tapered the wrong way! Even the jean companies now have men's jeans because they recognize the fact that middle-aged men are shaped differently from young men. You scrutinize every wrinkle. My wife, Carol Ann, informed me she's going to faithfully apply face cream to my face. Wrinkles begin to appear. Our stamina continues to lessen. Our physical abilities, once taken for granted, are on the wane—like eyesight and hearing. All of a sudden our faculties become weaknesses and not strengths. The mood of mid-life is characterized by dissatisfaction and disillusionment, disenchantment and boredom.

The two most common emotions we feel during these years are depression and self-pity. "Poor me." All of us are going to struggle with this. One of our young deacons once came in using a cane. "What in the world happened to you?" Playing tennis. Trying to stay young. Sitting before me on the second row was a member with crutches. He hurt his knee playing church softball. We have invented a whole new sport to cope with middle-age crisis. We call it slow-pitch softball. When I grew up we only threw fast pitch. The faster you could throw it, the better. Guess what? The young people have stolen slow pitch exactly like they did fast pitch.

Face it. You and I are not as young as we used to be and can't run with the kids anymore. "The old grey mare, she ain't what she used to be." For years, the PGA has sponsored a seniors' golf tour. Why? Because once you reach fifty, you can't hang in there with the twenty- and thirty-year olds. Old Bob Wills played, "Time changes everything." This is a time of graphic reality to us. We will not always have the opportunities we have today.

Here are the three distinct stages of aging, and how they relate. In youth we look to the future. In old age we look to the past, but in middle age we recognize that the goals that we had set, we must achieve *now*—or never. Time is limited, and we begin to focus in on right now. This is why so many middle-aged individuals are so vulnerable to mistakes—because they think they have to accomplish everything now. Solve it now, achieve it now, accomplish it now. While experiencing physical-emotional-attitudinal changes, the mid-lifer looks at the past and sees failures and unrealized dreams. When they consider the future, they envision only a continued deterioration of strength and old age, and often they become so preoccupied with past failures and future fears that they destroy the present. It is a most critical time of life.

The psalmist was exactly like that. In this psalm, he sings about this crisis, referring to being delivered out of his problems. He affirms in verse 5-6: "Thou art my hope, O Lord God: thou art my trust from my youth. By thee have I been held up from the womb: [from the very time of my conception I was held by your strength]." In verse 9 he prays, "Cast me not off in the time of old age; forsake me not when my strength faileth."

Zero in on verse 17: "O God, thou hast taught me from my youth." Then there is verse 18: "When I am old and grayheaded, O God forsake me not." He understood his mortality and his desperate need of God in that time. From his predicament he reached out to God for help. We mid-lifers can identify with that. Doctors report that at the point of birth the aging process begins to set in. We begin to die even as we begin to live. Certain functions begin to deteriorate even in a child because we are all in this process of physical and emotional change. That happens even to the Christian. There is no exemption from that.

I believe personally that much of the confusion, chaos, and unrest in our society is because we have put such a premium on youth and strength that our culture is now disintegrating. Soon there will be more retirees than teenagers. In only a few years over 50 percent of our population will be over fifty years of age. In our culture, though, many people are without foundation, without root, without mooring, without sources to guide them through the changing processes. The psalmist declares there are three things we need as we face the middle years of life. Jot these down in your heart as we dig into the seventy-first Psalm.

I. We Need the Protection of God

In the first three verses he wrote, "In thee, O Lord, do I put my trust: let me never be put to confusion. Deliver me in thy righteousness, and cause me to escape: incline thine ear unto me, and save me. Be thou my strong habitation, whereunto I may continually resort." Verse 4 continues, "Deliver me, O my God, out of the hand of the wicked." Verse 5—"For thou art my hope, O Lord God." Verse 6—"By thee have I been held up from the womb." Verse 7—"Thou art my strong refuge." Verse 8—"Let my mouth be filled with thy praise and with thy honor all the day." As we approach these uncertain middle years of life we need the protection of God for our lives.

There are three consoling facts about that protection.

The Comfort of God

First, God protects us by giving us comfort. He stresses that often through these first eight verses. The psalmist basically teaches that God deserves our confidence, and we ought to place our unwavering confidence in Him. You can trust God, so you ought to present your heart to Him. Put your life in His hands. Commit your all Him.

Then he makes a contrast. You must always guard against relying on the arm of flesh. "The arm of flesh will fail you, Ye dare not trust your own." As you age, you realize how feeble and weak you really are. The psalmist emphasizes we must rely on the comfort and strength of the Lord. He speaks of the Lord as being a "strong habitation." In other words, we ought to live under the protection of God all the time.

The Character of God

God is going to be true to His character. God is going to do what He promised He would do. In verse 8 he exults: "Let my mouth be filled with thy praise and with thy honor all the day." Matters will never turn sour if you keep your mouth full of praising the Lord. If you will fill your mouth with words of honor and praise to God, God will bless you. His *comfort* and *character* are protections for us.

The Conduct of God

Then he emphasizes that *the Lord's conduct* is also a protection. The psalmist testifies in verse 4 that God would deliver him— "out of the hand of the wicked, out of the hand of the unrighteous and cruel man,"—and that He would hold him and walk with him through life. All of these truths indicate that God's conduct lies in that He has done what we have asked Him to do.

The "cruel" man was a threat. The word *cruel* literally means "leavened" in the Hebrew. Leaven permeates a lump of dough. Most of the references to leaven in the bible refer to the fermentation and spreading of evil. God's protection guards us from the man who is "leavened" with hostility, anger, and viciousness toward God. When a man is hostile toward God, of course, he will be the same toward God's people. God's conduct is to protect us from cruel and wicked persons.

He speaks about God holding him from the womb. In essence he testified: Before I could even understand the power of God, that power sustained me. God knew us before we knew anything. Here is a beautiful play on the providential protection of God. In verse 6 he sings about God's providence guiding him from the time of conception in his mother's womb. In verses 5 and 17 he speaks about God guiding him through his youth, and in verses 9 and 18 he talks about God preserving him in old age. It is "healthy, wealthy, and wise" to give ourselves to God's available protection.

If we are going to grow old gracefully through the confusion, changing years of mid-life, we must have *the protection of God*.

II. We Need the Presence of God

The presence of God.—In verse 9, the psalmist says, "Cast me not off in the time of old age; forsake me not when my strength faileth." In relation to the presence of God he makes several profound assertions. We need *the companionship of God.* God needs to be more than a vague concept. Only if God is a companion can we work through these troublesome years of life. "How firm a foundation" with God as our companion. David was not tired of God, but he was afraid God might be tired of him. So in his frailty he cried, "O God, don't forsake me in the time of my old age." Old age robs us of personal strength and physical beauty, and we are not as able to serve God with the speed and strength we once had. When that happens, though, it does not diminish God's love and favor. God doesn't love us for what *we can do*—He loves us for what *He can do* in us.

Some clever wit has called the mature years, the "metallic years" —"silver in my hair, gold in my teeth, iron in my vitamins, and lead in my shoes." Many of us can identify with that. As we age there is an increasing sense of helplessness. Many fears include questions such as: Will we have sufficient funds to pay the bills? Who will take care of us if we are disabled? Is it safe to live alone? And we do not want to be put to shame; we do not want to grow old ungracefully. The desire of the psalmist's heart is that he might grow mellow but not grow rotten! One of the severe problems of age is often loneliness. Friends and family move or die, and we must often relocate, sometimes pulling up our roots and being transplanted. This creates extreme uneasiness. The psalmist advises, if you're going to grow old gracefully, you desperately need the companionship of God.

Another tendency as we grow older is impatience. I love verse 12. "O God, be not far from me: O my God, make haste for my help." In today's language he is insisting, "Lord, help me, and do it right now." Only the companionship of God in your life will overcome the lack of patience. Then in our hearts there will be *commendation from God.* Verses 14 and 15 speak of this. "I will hope continually, and will yet praise thee more and more. My mouth shall show forth thy righteousness and thy salvation all the day; for I know not the numbers thereof." Here is a declaration of what

God has done. When we have positive, fruitful, and satisfying experiences with God, it is natural for us to testify of those. That is the nature of our faith and the idea of hope.

Hope is a long and patient waiting in spite of delay or disappointment—the opposite of fear and dread. Scriptural hope for the Christian is not a self-produced feeling of encouragement that may be imaginary wishful thinking or a "hope-so" philosophy, but it is an anticipation built on the firm foundation of God's character and Word. Hope is not "iffy"—it is absolutely certain. It is not a case of "might be." It is and is to be the hope we have in the Lord Jesus Christ.

The Hebrew in verse 15 is interesting. "My mouth shall show forth." Some translations render it, "My mouth shall tell thy righteousness, and thy salvation all the day; for I know not the numbers thereof." That was almost the concept in the songwriter's mind when he wrote, "Count your many blessings, name them one by one." Commend to God for His blessings, for what He has done. Through this crisis period of our lives, we need the protection and presence of God.

Then he concludes by saying:

III. We Need the Power of God

The major thrust here is on a personal witness with others. God does not bless us merely for us to enjoy His blessings, but so we can be a blessing to other people. "I will go in the strength of the Lord God: I will make mention of thy righteousness, even of thine only" (v. 16). The emphasis of this passage is on the strength of God in our lives and how we are fortified by that power. We are responsible, then, for declaring the goodness and mercies of God.

In the covenant God made with Abram (before He changed his name to Abraham) God promised, "And I will make of thee a great nation, and I will bless thee, and make thy name great; and thou shalt be a blessing" (Gen. 12:2). God wants you and me to be blessings. Paul wrote in 2 Corinthians 1:3-4: "Blessed be God, even the Father of our Lord Jesus Christ, the Father of mercies, and the God of all comfort; Who comforteth us in all our tribulation, that we may be able to comfort them which are in any trouble, by the comfort wherewith we ourselves are comforted of God."

When God blesses us we are to "pass it on" to bless other people. We are stewards of the blessings of God and the hand of God upon our lives. Every encounter with God calls forth an urgency to be a blessing to other people. We can trust in the Lord because He is powerful. He is more than able to give us what we need. But for a person to have strength in the maturing years he should start early. You should not wait until old age to start laying a foundation for that period. I do not mean to suggest one cannot come to God in old age—it's never too late to come to God. But if you want to have a happy, fruitful mid-and-old-age, you must start sowing the seed *now*. There is nothing to compare with growing older with God. God will bless year by year.

Verse 18 reminds us that when our infirmities multiply, God will multiply the grace we need. Upon seeing others go through tragedy and travail, have you ever remarked, "Man, I couldn't endure what they did. I couldn't handle that"? No, you might not be able to handle it; but if you needed to, God would grant you the grace to do it. If you put your trust and faith in God and His Word, when that crisis does come, He will give you sustenance to see you through.

Nothing will cause God to forsake those who have not forsaken Him. God is not going to turn loose of you. In verse 18 notice the psalmist pledges to spend the rest of his life making God and His works known. He prays: "God, forsake me not; until I have showed thy strength unto this generation, and thy power to everyone that is to come." All of us should pray every day that as long as we live here, it will be our desire to declare the goodness and the grace of God. As you grow old, don't quit. Use your remaining time to glorify God and commit yourselves to Him. What a difference it would make if all of us entering our older years would determine to use every God-given moment to declare God's goodness.

Verse 19, a remarkable verse, says, "Thy righteousness also, O God, is very high, who hast done great things: O God, who is like unto thee?" The righteousness of God is high, pure, holy, and eternal. "God, who is like unto thee?" is a rhetorical question. Of course, the answer is nobody. God is totally incomparable. Commit your life to God, and you have tied into eternity, to that which is timeless, which is ageless, which is unchanging, and which is incorruptible. What a tremendous confirmation this is as we consider the power of God.

On the surface, verse 21 appears selfish: "Thou shalt increase my greatness, and comfort me on every side." In his mind he considered the troubles he had had and would have to face. It is really not a selfish verse. He was saying, "Lord, I want to thank You that whatever my trials, You are going to give me the strength to face them." Amid adversity, God will increase our coping ability. We must remember that we encourage others by how we handle crises. These verses assure us that God is in control of the crisis, but we all too easily forget that supportive fact. According to verse 20, God "shalt quicken me again, and shalt bring me up again from the depths of the earth." God will renew us even when we feel dead. The psalmist speaks about trusting in the Lord because He is indeed trustworthy, and then he concludes this psalm by offering thanksgiving to the Lord. "I will also praise thee with the psaltery, even thy truth, O my God: unto thee will I sing with the harp, O thou Holy One of Israel. My lips shall greatly rejoice when I sing unto thee; and my soul, which thou hast redeemed. My tongue also shall talk of thy righteousness all the day long: for they are confounded, for they are brought unto shame, that seek my hurt" (vv. 22-24).

The psalmist started out in verse 3 with a voice of praise. He was continually praising God. In verses 6, 8, 14-16, and 22, he extended his praise. His praise was not occasional, not intermittent, but continual and constant.

I repeat: We may have a tendency as we grow older to become critical and bitter and to spend our time complaining. How can you avoid that? Fill your mouth with the praises of God. Dwell on the good things God has done, and commit yourself to declaring those bountiful blessings. The psalmist had begun moaning because of his enemies, his misfortune, and the pressure exerted on him. Then he burst into a song of thanksgiving as he closed the psalm. You want to ask, "What happened to his enemies?" "What had changed?" Nothing, except that he was so preoccupied with the praises of God, he had no time to focus on his opposition. If we will occupy ourselves with the Lord, He will take care of our enemies. Fill your day with praise to God, and that praise will defeat your foes and lift your heart.

We need the protection, the presence, and the power of the Lord for these years.

You may not be going through a mid-life crisis or coming close to the retirement years, but you do need to start now laying the foundation to make your golden years happy years. Prepare to meet the Lord by faithfully doing His work each day. Then you will be ready when the time comes. The important matter is not that you add years to your life, but that you add life to your years! What will it profit a person if he lives a long time, and he's miserable and makes everybody else miserable? Determine now that we're not going to allow the river of our lives to end up in a swamp, but rather, as Jesus described, let there be rivers of living water gushing out of us that will bless those around us and be life-giving and life-sustaining. That's how we ought to move through the maturing years of life—building our lives on God, on our commitment to Him, tied deeply to the foundation of God's character and Word. As the years roll by, God will bless us with buoyancy, joy, and satisfaction as we share the goodness of God.

You can do more than survive the mid-life crisis. You can pass through it with victory, confidence, delight, and joy if you place God at the center of your life and dreams, and your ambitions are built upon Him.

8
Turning Tears into Rejoicing
Psalm 84

Psalm 84 is called a "Psalm of the Sanctuary." One of the subtitles indicates "A Psalm for the sons of Korah." The sons of Korah were Levites responsible for the services in the house of the Lord, in the tabernacle, and later in the temple. Apparently, the sons of Korah had been separated from the temple for an extended period. Somehow they had not been able to attend temple services. The reason might have been sickness or circumstances. Many think that this psalm was written immediately following the reign of Hezekiah and the attack of the Assyrians on Jerusalem. God had wrought a miracle when an angel had destroyed an Assyrian army of 185,000, slain in a single night as the people of Jerusalem trusted God.

Apparently that time had passed. God removed the threat, and there was free access to travel.

The setting of this psalm centers on pilgrims, separated from the temple, for a long time, who were en route to the temple. They were singing praises and rejoicing for the privilege of returning to the house of God. The services were to be restored, and the sons of Korah were once again assuming their leadership role. This "Song of the Sanctuary" is for us today. We can make this song our song as we think of the goodness of God in giving us a place to worship. This is a song of our gathering together week by week to worship God.

Truly, if you are saved you are going to love the place where God's people meet. This is also a song of praise and thanksgiving to God for what He has done in blessing us with a place of worship. Tucked away in the middle of the psalm is the text. "Who passing through the valley of Baca make it a well; the rain also filleth the pools" (v. 6). When one reads casually through this psalm, one is so overwhelmed with the beauty of the psalmist's love for the sanctuary and his praise to God, that one often misses this little verse.

The valley of Baca. Baca's root word is from a word which means "to weep." Baca is a valley of tears—a "vale of tears." Strangely, it is never translated weeping. I'm not sure why. Some have suggested that it refers—because of its similarity in the Hebrew language—to the balsam tree, and that tree thrives in the desert. It flourishes in dry, arid places.

Most scholars feel the psalmist has described a group of happy pilgrims passing through a parched desert. And surprisingly, many times during the night refreshing rains would fall, and when one woke up in the morning, the desert would be filled with water. Almost overnight the valley of Baca would be covered with lush greenery.

Often such a phenomenon occurs in Kenya. During the dry season it is barren and parched. Return several months later when the rains have fallen, and brown, desert-looking land will have been transformed into a lush carpet of green. In Tanzania, in deep woods, our guide struck a match and started a fire. I asked, "What in the world are you doing?" He replied, "I'm burning off the grass." It burned so fast it didn't even bother the trees. They burn the dry, brittle grass to prepare for the first rain.

As those singing pilgrims traveled through, they enjoyed refreshing rain, and the desert became a veritable garden paradise. This is the heart of this passage. They loved the sanctuary of God and His presence. Their real longing was not just for the place of worship, but for the God they worshiped. They replaced the weeping and despair of Baca with the joy of revived hearts. Those pilgrims not only endured the valley of weeping without losing heart, but they recreated that valley into a joyful scene of songs. God was so real, and their joy so genuine, their faces so radiant, their songs so uplifting, and their spirits so contagious that their passing through the valley made a vast difference. That is the heart of these verses.

This psalm divides itself into three distinct parts. The first is:

I. Praise

In verses 1-4 the psalmist praised God for His houses of worship and for His presence. This is the basis for his praise. "How amiable are thy tabernacles, O Lord of hosts! My soul longeth, yea, even fainteth for the courts of the Lord: my heart and my flesh crieth out for the living God" (vv. 1-2). Here was the heart's desire of the writer. As you look at these verses, you will note two central elements—first, *his love for the sanctuary*. He loved the house of God, a place where he could draw aside and worship God.

The place we call the church building is very special. Many evangelicals tend to denigrate the "church house." It is set apart for the worship of God—every church building for the worship of God is a testimony of the presence and majesty of God.

Second, there was *his longing for the sanctuary*. The living God was the true object of his longing and praise. The last portion of verse 2 goes, "My heart and my flesh cry out for the living God" (NIV). He was not merely loving the stone and the building materials in the house of worship. He was well aware that the building was only a means to an end. He went there so he could more purely, more specifically, more earnestly praise and worship the living God. That's what the building is all about. There's nothing sacred about the bricks, mortar, steel, wood, nails, and glass of a physical building. It is sacred because it was set apart for the purposes of God. The purpose of the building is to allow our entrance into an ever-deepening expression with the Lord Himself.

If I were afraid I had a high temperature, I would put a thermometer under my tongue for about three minutes, and it would indicate my temperature. If I were concerned about my blood pressure, I would have it checked. You want to know how your spiritual life is? I want to give you a test, and it's found right here. What do you really want? You can counterfeit everything else, even what you say. You can learn "the language of Zion," you can learn how to discuss theology; you can learn how to talk in a manner that makes you seem to be a spiritual person. You can fake that. You can learn to do religious things, going to church, sitting while the preacher talks instead of singing, "playing church." But you cannot fake your desires. Where and what are your desires? Your desires form the "acid test" of your spiritual life. You may answer, "Well, I'd like to have a better job, like to have more money, like to have better health." What do you want? The psalmist sang, "My heart cries for the living God. My heart longs for His sanctuary."

More than ever this is a day of excuses. Those who visit for the church and witness for Christ hear every conceivable kind of excuse and alibi. Many people are looking for an excuse not to enter the sanctuary. It's interesting—the people who criticize the organized church the most are those who are free to go and don't, but let someone be forced to stay away, and their hearts long for the fellowship of the people of God and for the sacred place of sanctuary. The desires and longings of the psalmist were centered in the sanctuary and the presence of the living God.

Demonstration of Praise

The demonstration of that praise is found in verses 3 and 4: "Yea, the sparrow hath found an house, and the swallow a nest for herself, where she may lay her young, even thine altars, O Lord of hosts, my King, and my God. Blessed are they that dwell in thy house: they will still be praising thee." The real point is: just like sparrows and swallows have freedom to enter a house or nest, so, too, may we find security and safety when we enter the house of God. When they come they are welcome. Virtually no one drives out the birds and tells them they cannot build their nests there. Even those little winged creatures find a sense of security and welcome. They have free access and feel at home.

Just as the birds are welcome in God's house, so am I. I have the same opportunity that the birds have—that sense of belonging and being at home. The church ought to be like that. We ought to feel at home when we gather together. We have a sense of responsibility to the family because we belong when we gather together. So the psalmist demonstrates the basis of his praise as he thinks first about his free access and then of the sheer delight of dwelling in the house of the Lord.

There are three blesseds in this Psalm—in verses 4, 5, and 12. *Blessed* here is not the usual word for blessed we find in relation to God. This is a word with a far broader meaning that really means exceedingly happy. Literally the text says, "O, happy is the man who settles down in Your house. He will be praising You continually." Here is a demonstration of praise, a spontaneous response of joy that leaps within the heart of the one who comes to praise the Lord. And that word *happy* is called "the plural of majesty." It just magnifies the meaning, and word for word it says: "Oh the great happiness, oh, how happy are those who dwell in the house of the Lord. They will continually be praising the Lord." So here is his praise.

Verses 5-7 speak of:

II. Provision

"Blessed is the man"—how happy is the man—"whose strength is in thee; in whose heart are the ways of them" (v. 5). The word *ways* literally means highways. In other words, the highways of our hearts—the thoughts and the emotions that travel up and down the highways of our hearts—are the ways of God. They are grounded in God Himself. Blessed. The provision God makes is that we receive strength in the paths of God in our hearts. In verses 6 and 7 he refers to going through the valley of Baca and finding a well there and rains filling the pool and going from strength to strength. All of them in Zion appear before God. The provision of God.

Verse 5 teaches us that in God's provision there is refreshing. "Blessed is the man whose strength is in thee; in whose heart are the ways of them." There is a natural bridge of thought from those who love the sanctuary to the blessings they will receive. For those who love the Lord, desire His presence, and rejoice in the opportunity to dwell in and to worship in His sanctuary, there are distinct benefits and blessings. When the Lord Himself is your priority, blessings will flow.

First, of course, the chief object is the Lord Himself. He meets the worshiper there. The richest blessing is that when we pour our hearts out to God, He is there. God is not hiding from us. "Seek ye the Lord while he may be found, call ye upon him while he is near" (Isa. 55:6). "Thou shalt seek the Lord thy God, thou shalt find him, if thou seek him with all thy heart and with all thy soul" (Deut. 4:29). "If you seek Me," God promises, "you will find Me." What does that mean? That means you have as much of God right now as you want! From the refreshment springing from the provision of God we find strength and direction for our lives.

Then verses 6 and 7 made it clear that there is restoration in God's provision for us, who are passing through the valley of weeping. Have you ever been there? Have you ever walked through a desert place? Have you ever gone through a time of weeping, of grief, or assault on your life? When you pass through the valley of Baca you will make it a well. What a thrilling picture is here. Like the pilgrims you can brighten the day, bless the day. Life can be like a parched valley. But have you noticed, some have the capacity to refresh the place where they are? The old song goes, "Brighten the corner where you are."

I often commented that there's too much week between Sundays. I love Sundays. It's a gala happening when we gather together. There is often barrenness when we are not together. We all pass through those desert places. The key is: how do we go through them?

How well we remember the story of the good Samaritan. In a desert place, a man had been beaten, robbed, and left for dead. Here came a priest, a big-time preacher going to a meeting. He saw the man in desperate need, but he passed by. The Levite came along behind him. The custodian of the law, he guarded and protected the Scriptures of God, but he looked on the man and left him there. Those two passed through the man's valley and made no difference at all. Then the Samaritan came and moved into action. He nursed his wounds, put him on his own means of transportation, and carried him to a place of safety and healing. He brightened the valley. He lifted the gloom. Thank God, there are a lot of folks like him.

John Bunyan was languishing in Bedford Prison in London, jailed for preaching. It was a dreadful place to be—separated from his family. All he had to do was recant and agree not to preach about Jesus, but he remained firm. He could have written a book wrapped in self-pity, expressing bitterness, despair, and complaint to God. Instead he wrote the *Pilgrim's Progress*, which has sold more copies in English than any other book in the world except the Bible. Who could forget that moment when Christian, the hero of the story—after carrying the heavy weight of his sins he had never been able to shake—finally climbed up Calvary stumbling and straining until he fell on his knees before that cross? The burden rolled from his shoulders and down the hill of Calvary until it disappeared into an empty tomb! John Bunyan walked through the valley of weeping and dryness and yet delivered joy and refreshing.

Robert Browning wrote a poem about a little girl named Pippa who worked in a sweatshop. On her way to work she passed through a ghetto of doom and despair. As she walked through that neighborhood that reeked of hopelessness and grief, Pippa sang. As she sang from her heart the shutters flew open, and it seemed that the sunlight once again shone because Pippa brightened the valley through which she passed.

Our Lord Jesus is a perfect example of that, isn't He? Blind Bartimaeus was in the valley of physical impairment, his personal Baca, but Jesus walked through and gave him sight. Zacchaeus had his valley of Baca, bound by his own pride and greed—Jesus walked through that man's valley and gave him eternal life.

Description of God's People

I could also speak of Mary Magdalene, Simon Peter, the Gadarene demoniac (Legion). A classic example is the woman at the well in Sychar, Samaria. Jesus walked through her valley of isolation and desperation, and new life came to her heart and revival to her community because Jesus came through. Notice the phrase "from strength to strength," the description of God's people going through the valley of Baca.

Face it. You and I are going to walk through our valley and many other valleys. What are we going to do? Will we add to the gloom, or will we create joy where there was weeping and refreshing where there was desert? We can go from strength to strength. I think of going through a stream, jumping from rock to rock. Miss the rock, and you fall. That was vividly demonstrated to me when we were on the Susitna River in Alaska. When the river is at flood stage it covers an unbelievable amount of territory. Even in the fall at low ebb it was vast and wide. This huge river had cut channels through the land. When the water was down these channels were filled with stagnant water and quicksand, but we had to cross it.

We emerged from the brush one day, and were on the bank of a channel, and as far as we could see, there was nothing but debris and driftwood, and down below was stagnant water. We leaped from log to log, looking down sometimes six, eight, and ten feet below. We didn't want to be there. I was glad we could go from strength to strength. Life is like that. When you love the Lord with all your heart, and you long for the house of God and His presence, there will be light in the valley, refreshing in the desert.

The last section of this psalm deals with:

III. Prayer

"O Lord God of hosts, hear my prayer: give ear, O God of Jacob. Selah" (v. 8). He calls God "Lord God of hosts." That speaks of the plentitude of His power. The Lord God of hosts governs all the universe, directs all of the heavenly bodies, and manages every force in this universe of His. This speaks of His strength, His might, His ability to meet our needs. We quickly run out of adjectives referring to the Almighty God. The God of Jacob relates to the God who aided Jacob when he didn't deserve it—when Jacob was a backslider, a slanderer, a treacherous liar and deceiver. The God of Jacob is merciful. As Jacob we pray to God who has strength to answer and who has grace and mercy. What a tremendous truth!

First of all, the prayer involves service. I like that because we often talk about "putting feet to our prayers." This is what happened here. "Behold, O God our shield, and look upon the face of thine anointed. For a day in thy courts is better than a thousand. I had rather be a doorkeeper in the house of my God, than to dwell in the tents of wickedness" (vv. 9-10). The sons of Korah also had the service of being doorkeepers, as it were, in the temple of God. There is ecstatic joy in serving God in His house. The roots and fruitfulness of godly lives are traced to the sanctuary. You may ask, "Are you saying that I can't serve God apart from the sanctuary?" No, but if you truly serve God it will include the sanctuary. Nowhere in Scripture are you instructed to forsake the assembling of yourselves together. The opposite is true (see Heb. 10:25). Our church buildings are testimonies to the fact that the people of God started a church and over the years they have been true and faithful to God, in spite of many struggles and heartaches. Every Bible-believing, gospel-preaching church declares that His people love God and His house and want the world to receive that gospel. One may go on and serve apart from the church if one likes, but one will not do it scripturally. The person away from God's house will always have a nagging awareness that something is wrong.

You might alibi: "But I don't think everything is done like it ought to be." Of course not. Why should that surprise you? I have a new survey. *One out of one persons is a sinner.* Why, then, do you expect perfection out of sinners? Sure there's some difficulty in every church. It's because we're here. Now if we weren't, somebody else would be, and the problems would still exist. We don't come together because we have all the wrinkles ironed out and all the problems solved—but because when we come together, we draw strength from one another, and as we praise God He gives new life to us. Praise God for the privilege of serving Him.

Notice he wrote, "I'd rather be a doorkeeper in the house of [the Lord] than to dwell in the tents of wickedness." A day in God's court is better than a thousand outside days. Every time I come to church on Sunday I think of this verse. The joy of doing even the "chores" in the house of the Lord is better than a thousand days elsewhere. It's sad, though, that many spend most of their time trying to find that something else, don't they?

People still use the cliché: "When my ship comes in." If it comes in, they won't like it. If it does, they'll want another ship. If they did "what comes naturally," "what feels good," for a thousand days, it wouldn't compare to one day of opening a door at God's house. Now etch this on the tables of your heart. There are no menial jobs in the kingdom of God. The doorkeeper's job, I believe, is just as important as that of teachers and preachers.

Verses 11 and 12 refer to the *satisfaction* we enjoy when we desire with all of our hearts to know him. "For the Lord God is a sun and shield: the Lord will give grace and glory: no good thing will he withhold from them that walk uprightly." If you feel God is keeping the good from you, examine your own heart. He will give you everything good. Now good in God's eyes may not always seem good in ours. God blesses those who keep coming into His presence— grace and glory, favor and honor.

"Sun and shield" (v. 11) means positive protection from fear and defeat. The answer is military. Why would we need a shield if we weren't in a battle? Maybe the reason you may be frustrated in your spiritual life is that you are hurt in spiritual warfare. We were intended to be in the battle, so God gave us a shield, not to hang on the wall and admire, but to use as a defense against the devil.

Yes, God has promised to be with us always, but that is not unconditional. Even in the Great Commission, the condition is: He will be with us when we go and carry the message. God especially blesses the church or person who is obedient to His commands. God never promised to bless *our* plans, *our* programs unless we are intent about His business. Our shield of protection is in our obedience to God. As we come to and from the sanctuary we pass through many dread valleys.

The answer is found in the three "blesseds" in this psalm. "Blessed is the man whose strength is in thee; in whose heart are the ways of them" (v. 5). "Blessed is the man that trusteth in thee" (v. 12). It was not just the sanctuary that was so significant, but also the man who came to the sanctuary in this psalm. If we are going to be used of God to turn tears into rejoicing and make the desert place resplendent with springs and refreshing rain, we must live close to God.

The answer really is that when Jesus Christ lives in us, we catch His spirit and reflect His attitude. When Jesus is in control of our lives, we will turn tears into joy going toward the sanctuary. Praise God for Sundays, but also thank God for the valleys, the dry places, the grief periods. Bless God for what He does in our lives as we are going to God's house.

9
Overwhelmed with Loneliness
Psalm 102

The notes in the *King James Version* refer to Psalm 102 as: "A Prayer of the afflicted, when he is overwhelmed, and poureth out his complaint before the Lord." Yes, this psalm blends together the psalmist's grief and sorrow for his nation and himself. Like many servants of God, he felt as if he were the only one who cared and prayed for his country. Personal grief, suffering, and loneliness pour out in his petition. His personal, private troubles are later transcended by his concern for the destiny of Israel. The promised glory of Zion seems to be painfully slow in fulfillment.

His sufferings are unexplained. He gives no rationale for the pressure and pain he describes. The miseries in his nation, however, cause him far more anguish than his own personal problems. The prayer of this psalm is more in spirit than in word. In the first eleven stanzas, there are moanings of grief and confessions of faith gushing from his spirit—there is a sort of grasping as he expresses his suffering and sorrow.

So this psalm is one of *desolation*—loneliness—but it could also be described as one of *consolation*. There is the reality of his suffering but also the reality of God's presence, who gave him victory amid that suffering. Somewhere in every psalm we will find ourselves. The first 11 verses comprise what I would call *the psalmist's plight*. Verses 12-22 are *the psalmist's praise,* and verses 23-28 are *the psalmist's persuasion*.

First, look at:

I. The Psalmist's Plight

The text describes his prayers. "Hear my prayer, O Lord, and let my cry come unto thee. Hide not thy face from me in the day when

I am in trouble; incline thine ear unto me: in the day when I call answer me speedily" (vv. 1-2). In these two verses alone there are five petitions asking, "Lord, listen to me. Don't hide Your face from me. When I call on You, answer me right away." The fact he asks God to hear him does not imply he thinks God does not or will not.

The implication here is not that the psalmist feared God might not hear him, but rather his petition was an effective means of recalling that God is always ready to hear. He cries, "Lord, don't turn away from me. Now hear my prayer." He appeals to the God he trusts will hear. In whatever predicament we're in, whatever we're facing, God is always ready to respond. God is more than prepared to handle any sincere prayer.

Many times, though, our sin and rebellion separate us from the hand of God in our lives. Isaiah declared,

> Behold, the Lord's hand is not shortened, that it cannot save; neither his ear heavy, that it cannot here: But your iniquities have separated between you and your God, and your sins have hid his face from you, that he will not hear (Isa. 59:1-2).

God is always ready to hear the penitent cry, the desperate prayer of one who reaches out with all one's heart to God. It is wonderful to know that we have at least one friend who hears and understands, one who empathizes with us, suffers with us, listens to us. But how much better it is to realize that God Himself hears.

Verses 3-7 focus on his *predicament*. This is one of the most vivid, graphic descriptions anywhere in the Scriptures. He described fever, frailty, wasting, pain, sleeplessness, melancholy, rejection, despair, depression—it's all there. He spelled out his desperation. He felt as though he had been cursed by God. He was aware that God was not causing this, and yet it was almost as though he were alienated from God as he described his predicament. He did not attribute his affliction either to his sin or as a punishment for sin. How does he describe himself? "For my days are consumed like smoke, and my bones are burned as an hearth." The description of being "consumed like smoke" depicts dark, defiling, blinding, depressing situations, as if he were wandering in a dense fog. Have you ever been in a fire or been almost overcome by smoke? It is absolutely stifling. It is a dark, desperate experience.

"My bones are burned as an hearth." If his affliction were illness, perhaps this is a trenchant description of fever wracking a body. He felt his bones were like spent ashes ready to blow away. His spirit seemed dried up, wasted with anxiety. His lament continued, "My heart is smitten, and withered like grass; so that I forget to eat my bread" (v. 4). In his withered condition, he even forgot to eat. As with many depressed persons, he had lost his appetite. He was consumed with his concern that God would move, both in his nation and in his own life.

Verse 5 continues this extreme emotion: "By reason of the voice of my groaning my bones cleave to my skin." Here is a picture of advanced malnutrition. He was emaciated with sorrow and had become a living skeleton. His bones were so weak they couldn't drag the rest of his body around. Then he moved beyond his physical condition to his emotional experience. "I am like a pelican of the wilderness: I am like an owl of the desert. I watch, and am as a sparrow alone upon the housetop" (vv. 6-7).

I believe he was painting a picture of a person who felt absolutely abandoned, cut off. I remember lone pelicans in the African desert, silhouetted by themselves against the sunset. A pelican can be a mournful, ludicrous object, an image of desolation and isolation. The owl also seems to want solitude. Owls are often seen moping among the ruins, as it were. The screech or hoot of an owl is eerie and lonely. These two birds are commonly referred to in Scriptures as emblems of gloom and wretchedness. The psalmist pointed to himself as one who felt no one else cared.

In verse 7 he wrote: "I am like a sparrow alone upon the housetop." He considered himself the lone sentry for his nation. His peers were too selfish, too careless to watch. While he was undergoing these emotions and traumas, he also had heartfelt concern for the nation. How many of us are that concerned about America? The question is a rhetorical question, and obviously the answer is "few of us."

Beyond that, however, I wonder how many of us can identify with that description of his predicament? Isolated. Lonely. Cut off. Our insides are churning, our hearts are hurting. I cannot forget reading the account of a woman who died in a New York apartment complex right off the freeway that runs through Manhattan.

You could live and die and never leave the building where she lived. But the woman was not heard from for several days. Finally, the landlord went in and found her dead in her apartment. She had written on her diary every page for that year these three words—*no one came!* Can you identify with that? At one point or another, each of us experiences these emotions. We feel as though we are the only one who cares and hurts.

In verse 8 he wails, "Mine enemies reproach me all the day; and they that are mad against me are sworn against me." His enemies were unrelenting, unceasing, venting their taunts and ridicule on the psalmist's patriotism and griefs. Verse 8 indicates they had taken an oath to destroy him. They used him as a curse word—a synonym for hatred and contempt. When one stands for the cause of Christ in the nation, there will be plenty of the devil's people to attack and persecute.

Verse 9 is the first evidence we have of repentance. Until this point we have seen no sign of repentance on his part. Certain scholars claim there is no evidence of repentance anywhere in the psalm. "For I have eaten ashes like bread, and mingled my drink with weeping." The imagery touches on the practice of donning sackcloth and sprinkling ashes on one's head, an expression of repentance, humility, confession, and commitment to God. Apparently he had heaped ashes on his head until they had mingled with his food, and he ate food that tasted like ashes. His tears had mixed with his drink until it was brackish.

This is clear evidence of his repentance, his turning and reaching out to God. God always honors genuine repentance. His worst distress, though, was the feeling that God had exalted him and then thrown him down. "Because of thine indignation and thy wrath: for thou hast lifted me up and cast me down" (v. 10). Did you ever feel like that? Even in our relationship with God it is terrible to feel as if God Himself has cast us away.

The psalmist was not bitter toward God because he understood that the nation's sin had caused God to react with anger. God loves the sinner, but He hates the sin. When there is rebellion, God reacts with His wrath and His anger. God's anger is not an emotion— it's a settled condition. It is not an emotion at all. When we become angry we have an emotional upheaval. God's anger is not a fleeting emotion fueled by an outburst. God hates sin. God's wrath toward sin is bound up in His character. God's ways are not our ways. God always responds to sin with His wrath. "Be not deceived; God is not mocked: for whatsoever a man soweth, that shall he also reap. (Gal. 6:7).

That's written into the very fabric of our lives, and no one will ever get away with sin. "Be sure your sin will find you out" (Num. 32:23). Automatic in the character and nature of God is a holy hatred of sin, which brings His response. The psalmist felt bound up in the nation's sin to the extent he moaned, "My days are like a shadow that declineth" (v. 11a). Now a shadow would be bad enough, but a shadow on the decline is one that is going away. "And I am withered like grass" (v. 11b). He has depicted his *predicament* and his *persecution*. These first eleven verses are a harrowing account of one who desperately needed the touch of God on his life.

Verse 12 marks a turning point in the psalm. "But thou, O Lord" is crucial. "But thou, O Lord" starts one of the most beautiful songs of praise ever heard. Now we behold:

II. The Psalmist's Praise

He praises God for His righteous rule as he begins this passage. "Thou, O Lord, shalt endure forever." The words "shalt endure" literally mean *"shall sit enthroned."* God is seen sitting securely on His throne. He will sit forever. He has all things perpetually under His control.

Verse 13 is a cry especially from earth's perspective, but somehow it seems as if God's timetable is meshing with the situation. "Thou shalt arise, and have mercy upon Zion: for the time to favor her, yea, the set time, is come." The psalmist prays, "Lord, it's time for you to act. The fullness of time is approaching. There is no time to waste." There is a sense in which the timetable of God and man seems to be coming together in this declaration.

"For thy servants take pleasure in her stones," speaking of Zion, "and favor the dust thereof" (v. 14). This was a good sign. The captives began to feel homesick, and the remnant returned to rebuild and to give attention to the things of God. Mount Zion was lying in rubble, but the people became concerned about the stones and even the dust of the debris. So I relate this today. The greatest hope of the church is when the members become deeply involved in all that concerns the church, when they become gravely concerned that we be all that God has put us here to be.

So the psalmist treats the rule of God. When God moves in the hearts of His people, it builds up Zion. When that happens, verse 15 declares: "So the heathen shall fear the name of the Lord, and all the kings of the earth thy glory." It is sad that so little is happening among God's people that the world doesn't have much to behold.

You remember the recycled story about the church building being on fire. The backslider that had long been absent and the old man of the streets who never had been to church were watching it burn, and someone remarked, "Man, you haven't been coming to this church." One of the men quipped, "Yeah, but the church hasn't been on fire!"

When the church is on fire for God, folks will come and watch her burn. When God begins to move in the hearts of His people, and world will sit up and take notice. The worst tragedy in America today is that, by and large, the world ignores the church. But when Zion's servants take pleasure in her stones, and even favor its dust, "The heathen shall fear the name of the Lord, and all the kings of the earth [will notice] thy glory."

Quite frankly, I'd rather be attacked than ignored. I would rather the world be antagonistic toward the church than indifferent toward it. It would be marvelous if the lost world would exclaim, as it has before, "My, how those people love each other; how they care for others; how they touch lives; how they minister," and that word will get around. That's the picture we have here.

Beginning in verse 16 he praises God for the restoration: "When the Lord shall build up Zion, he shall appear in his glory." Here is the excited anticipation that climaxes in verse 22 with a description of the great, golden age of the millennial kingdom of Christ when all the kingdoms of the world will gather to serve the Lord. This is a messianic, eschatological discourse. What a glorious expectation! "Jesus shall reign where e'er the sun does its successive journeys run; His kingdom spread from shore to shore, Til moons shall wax and wane no more."

In verse 17 we have the promise that God establishes His glory in Zion. He will hear the prayer of the destitute. Earthly monarchs and leaders don't have time for "little" people, but God never loses interest in those who are poor and helpless. We have a God who will not treat any plea with contempt. God is interested in whatever our hearts cry for.

Verse 18 is a timely reminder of how we ought to train our children. "This shall be written for the generation to come." Literally, the word "generation" means a people yet unborn. We are to perpetuate the faithfulness of God. Our children need to know where we have come from and where they have come from. Our society is rearing a generation that does not know the Lord—that has no heritage, no legacy. The unborn generations yet to come need to know what God is doing. The best heritage we could leave our children is an understanding of God's reality in our lives so they may be aware of God's moving in theirs.

Verses 19 and 20 again emphasize the willingness of God to hear. "He hath looked down from the height of his sanctuary; from heaven, . . . To hear the groaning of the prisoner, to loose those that are appointed to death." How God cares! He relieves extreme distress. He breaks the chains of bondage that bind us, that restrict us, that enslave us. He responds to those groanings.

Verses 21 and 22 describe the golden age of restoration. In these verses are *the psalmist's praise.* He also wrote about *his plight.* Then he cried out, "But thou, O Lord" (v. 12). It all hinges on his awareness of the Lord.

And so we approach these last five verses to hear:

III. The Psalmist's Persuasion

Notice two truths. First is *his confidence.* In verse 23 he reverted to a mournful, personal complaint: "He weakened my strength in the way; he shortened my days." In other words, he was still having difficulties. So he burst forth with, "O my God, take me not away in the midst of my days: thy years are throughout all generations" (v. 24). In essence he said, "I still have weaknesses and problems. They haven't all been resolved or removed. But I have confidence in You, God."

I believe with all of my heart that the answer to our needs is an unquestioned faith and confidence in God. "All things work together for good to them who love God" (Rom. 8:28).

You say, "Preacher, how can you say everything is good?"

I didn't say everything was good, but that everything works together for good to the believer. God said it. I don't understand it, but I can believe it. "Cast not away therefore your confidence," Hebrews 10:35 states. "Don't lose heart in God." He had confidence that God could still strengthen and lengthen the days of his earthly life.

Godly people don't dread death, but there is nothing wrong with loving life. Some people think in order to be "spiritual" and godly one must despise life and live for a world yet to come. I believe that God wants us to enjoy the abundant, full life with fulfillment of all the deepest longings of our hearts. While we face death unafraid, we are not to be soured on life. I'm having a ball! I thank God for what He's up to. I thank God for where He's headed. I thank God that I've already read the last chapter in the Book, and I know how it's going to come out!

I do not dread death nor do I fear life. What better remedy is there for us than to take the loneliness, depression, and persecution we feel and reach out to God? That is the ultimate answer for all of us.

Now he declared *his conviction* in these last four verses. God is still the Creator God. Look at verses 25-27, "Of old thou hast"—by the way, this is almost literally quoted in Hebrews 1:10-12. "Of old thou hast laid the foundation of the earth: and the heavens are the work of thy hands. They shall perish, but thou shalt endure: yea, all of them shall wax old like a garment; [all the heavens] as a vesture shalt thou change them, and they shall be changed: But thou art the same, and thy years shall have no end."

His conviction is that we still have God as a Creator God. The psalmist was passing away, but God was and is. God is immutable, unchanging. The visible creation—even the sun, moon, and stars—the most fixed bodies in our universe, are changing. They are growing old and someday will wear out, but God will never wear out, never decay, never deteriorate, never be destroyed. None of the destructive forces that will ultimately change everything else can affect God.

Some feel that that last statement—"Thou art the same, and thy years have no end"—also may underline the thought in Hebrews 13:8: "Jesus Christ the same yesterday, and today, and forever." In this psalm there is a man in a terrible predicament. Under heavy persecution physically and emotionally, he was strung out. Physically he had little strength. Emotionally he had no stamina. Discouraged, in despair, concerned for both himself and for his nation, persecuted by his enemies who had sworn to destroy him, he had nothing else to do but turn to God. He turned to the God who would meet him at the point of his need, who would hear him, who would respond to him.

We sort of laugh at ourselves, and we comment, "When all else fails, *read the instructions.*" Did you ever try to assemble this or that; then after you messed it up, you said, "Well, I guess I'd better read the instructions." Right? When all else fails, turn to God. Only better: turn to God first. Do not wait until everything else fails. Nothing else is going to work. It doesn't matter what we try; there is an insatiable hunger in every one of our hearts.

Why do you think people turn to sex, drugs, alcohol, defiling habits, or immorality? Because there's something inside of us that longs for fulfillment and satisfaction. There's nothing wrong with that longing. God put that desire in our hearts, but only He can give you that satisfaction and meaning. Only He can give you purpose, and you can experientially spend your life proving that nothing else will work, or you can merely accept and acknowledge it. You don't have to mess up your life. You don't have to go deeper in sin. You don't have to twist and warp your life as others do. It doesn't have to become worse than it is. You've gone as far as you need to go. You don't need to experiment anymore, trying to find meaning and purpose in life. Whatever you try is not going to work. But if you will turn to God, you will find that all else your heart longs to experience will be found in Him.

Jesus presented the story of the prodigal son, a wayward, rebellious young man. What has always intrigued me about the story is that everything the son left home to find, he found when he came home. You will save yourself tremendous grief and despair if you will just confess, "Lord, I accept Your Word. I know You don't change. Everything else is going to wear out and give way, but You are unchanging. You are the same. I know that nothing else I try is going to bring meaning and joy to my life. Hear me, O Lord, when I pray. Let my cry come to You. Don't hide Your face from me when I'm in trouble. Incline Your ear to me in the day when I call. Answer me quickly."

When that becomes your cry in your loneliness, your emotional and physical trauma, your isolation that consumes you, God will be there to meet you at that point. But God is a gentleman. God never forces His way into your life. God is not going to slap you down and declare, "I'm coming to take over." You must open your heart to Him. Jesus promised that if anyone would hear His voice and open the door, He would come in. He will respond if we will only open the door!

10
Cultivating the Spirit of Gratitude

Psalm 116

Psalm 116 is a psalm of thanksgiving and gratitude. My thesis is that you have only two options. You will either cultivate a spirit of gratitude or a spirit of rebellion, of hostility. As we study our rebellious nature we discover that our ingratitude makes us rebellious.

Show me a grateful child, and you will have an obedient child. Show me a rebellious teenager, and you will have an ungrateful teenager. Look at an angry, hostile father, mother, husband, and/or wife, and you will see a person who has ingratitude in his/her life. Gratitude is a spirit that must be cultivated in our lives, sweetening our disposition, brightening our day, giving us a foundation on which to build a healthy and wholesome life.

If we do not cultivate the spirit of gratitude, we will gradually become arrogant and proud, demanding this or that which we have no right to demand. The truth is, all of us are more blessed than we deserve. If we received what we deserved, it would be genuinely sad. It would be bad news. We ought to be truly grateful, thankful people, knowing that "every good gift and every perfect gift comes down from the Father, in whom there is neither variableness nor shadow of turning" (Jas. 1:17). Gratitude. It is a godly characteristic, an attitude that is spiritual. This psalm concerns the intimate love of the psalmist whose heart is so filled with gratitude and overflowing with thanksgiving to God for his personal experience of redemption. The overriding theme is the thanksgiving that floods the soul when we realize all God has done for us. Notice how the psalm starts.

Four words are filled with all the meaning that we could possibly imagine. "I love the Lord..." It is a hallowed declaration that ought to be characteristic of every believer. All of us ought to be able to testify from our hearts: I love the Lord! Through our disappointments, sorrows, afflictions, sufferings, pain, and every experience there ought to be the glad, joyful declaration of our spirits—I love the Lord.

The psalmist confessed that he loved the Lord because of what He had done for him. That is so consistent with the apostle John who wrote: "We love him because he first loved us" (1 John 4:19). A genuine believer cannot help but love the Lord because of His responsiveness to us. He has stooped down to touch our lives. God's provisions are acts of His grace. God's grace causes Him to touch our lives and to provide for our needs. No wonder John Newton called it "Amazing Grace." It is absolutely amazing that God loves but also that He allows us to love Him. God lets us wrap our hearts around Him in love.

In these first two verses there are three tenses—present, past, and future. "I love the Lord"—present tense. "Because he hath heard my voice and my supplications, he hath inclined his ear unto me"—past tense. "Therefore I will call upon him as long as I live"—future tense. When we love the Lord we want to express it; we want people to know it; we want to make that love public. That train of thought runs throughout this entire psalm.

The psalmist has "fallen in love" with God, and he declares his total commitment to Him. This reveals what love will do in a person's heart. If you genuinely love God, you will think, act, and speak accordingly to express that love. This psalm illumines the pattern of love as it is expressed in our lives, and here is a touching word of thanksgiving, which I cannot read without my own heart being overwhelmed with gratitude for God's blessings to my family and me. I am inclined to remember Paul's phrase, "For the love of Christ constraineth us; . . ." (2 Cor. 5:14a). Gratitude to God compels us to express in word, thought, and deed how deeply we love Him. The bottom line in our relationship with God is our love for the Lord.

When the resurrected Christ was restoring Simon Peter, after Simon had denied his Lord three times, the Lord didn't ask Simon about his creed, his faithfulness, his activities. But three times He asked, "Simon, do you love Me?" (see John 21). The most important thing you can do is to love the Lord—just love Him. Let Him be your God; let Him stir your heart. Love Him. After all, loving God is the first and great commandment (see Matt. 22:37-38).

The Psalm distinctly divides into three sections. The first section deals with:

I. The Prayer of the Psalmist

In verses 1-8, he had been on the verge of death, and from the depths of pain and weakness he sought God's help. God's mercy and grace provided the answer. He discovered what all seeking believers sooner or later come upon, and that is: our God hears and answers prayer. All we are able to grasp about God, other than what we read in the Scriptures, we know as a result of answered prayer. Thus, the first section of this psalm digs into the matter of prayer. In the first two verses he points out what I would call the *perception of God.* "I love the Lord, because he hath heard my voice and my supplications. Because he hath inclined his ear unto me, therefore will I call upon him as long as I live." This type of exchange appears throughout the psalms: the psalmist cries to God, and the Lord hears and responds to his difficulties. That little phrase "inclined his ear" means more than merely hearing one's words. It implies that He not only heard the words, but He hurried to step into the situation. It was not a question of whether God hears our prayers, for God not only hears but also responds to our prayers.

Then the writer spoke of the pain he experienced. "The sorrows of death compassed me, and the pains of hell gat hold upon me: I found trouble and sorrow" (v. 3). He found dread, distress. "Then called I upon he name of the Lord; O Lord, I beseech thee, deliver my soul" (v. 4). "The sorrows of death" in the Hebrew showed a fierce aggression. That benumbing phrase carries the idea that death is searching after people, clutching after mankind, moving perniciously to waste life with sickness or to crush it with depression. The psalmist meant that the pressures of death were squeezing the life out of him. In spite of the stress and pain, though, he loved the Lord. Whether or not we suffer does not divide the spiritually minded from the fleshly minded, committed Christians from rebellious individuals.

Sometimes certain Christians have the idea that if only we would live right, we would never suffer. Not so. We are involved in a "body of death," as Paul called it. The moment we are born, we start dying. That is basic to our physical being. Since sin in Eden, "death passed upon all men, for that all have sinned" (Rom. 5:12b). It is a miracle of God's grace that we live as long as we do. If you will study Bible history and the Christian movement, there never was an elite group without trouble. You will be impressed with those who called upon the Lord in the midst of trouble.

The difference between individuals is not whether or not we suffer pain but what we do with the pain. How do we react to it? Underlying the emphasis of the Hebrew words, there was the concept of being caught, like an animal, in a hunter's trap. It was as though death itself were the hunter and the psalmist were the animal. In addition, the words "trouble and sorrow" in the original language described walls closing in on a person. The psalmist was "at wit's end row." Did you ever feel as though the ceiling was falling, the floor was moving up, the walls were closing in, and you were going to be squashed? All of those aforementioned feelings were his. In the midst of all that he cried unto the Lord. He was on the edge of the precipice, in the strong grip of disease, bowed in anguish and grief, broken and lonely, and almost without hope. He literally screamed unto the Lord. From *pain* he *prayed*.

Then pay attention to verses 5-8. They deal with:

II. The Protection of the Psalmist

"Gracious is the Lord, and righteous..." These two words, gracious and righteous, are not used together often. Then he added a third word—*merciful*. God is a God of grace, of justice, righteousness, mercy, and compassion. Those are remarkable words speaking of what God does. God is righteous, gracious in hearing us, righteous in judging us, merciful in forgiving us, and righteous in rewarding us above and beyond our just desserts. He gives us the benefit of every good thing that may ever enter our lives. The bottom line is: because of His goodness and godliness God blesses us in spite of our lack of righteousness. "Gracious is the Lord, and righteous; yea, our God is merciful" (v. 5).

Not only that, the inspired writer continued: "The Lord preserveth the simple: I was brought low, and he helped me" (v. 6). You could interpret "simple" to mean people who have childlike trust and faith. Of course, God does watch over those who trust Him like that. Sometimes the Hebrew word was used in reference to those gullible, naïve people who are always in trouble. Kids are sometimes like that. Many have a knack for being in the wrong place at the wrong time. Another definition of the simple could be those who are so simple that they do not have profound understanding. Sometimes those with learning disabilities have such a simplicity about them, they do not easily understand.

Yet, the wonderful truth here is that God preserves even the simple, gullible, naïve folks. The psalmist is careful and humble in identifying with those people, and God is gracious in looking out for them. If you don't think you need God, and you don't have time for Him, and if you're too smart for Him, he can do nothing for you. But if you are patently simple enough to realize you need God, He will respond to your needs. When out of helplessness and sheer simplicity you recognize that all you have and are depends on Him, and you cry out to Him, God has a word for you—then He can move in your life.

"I was brought low, and he helped me" (v. 6b). That means he was "drained dry." He was helpless, and because he was helpless, God would help him. "Return unto thy rest, O my soul; for the Lord hath dealt bountifully with thee. For thou hast delivered my soul from death, mine eyes from tears, and my feet from falling" (vv. 7-8). Beginning in verse 9 a *promise* is made, and it starts off with a *pledge*: "I will walk before the Lord in the land of the living." He makes it plain—he is totally sold out to the Lord. He loves the Lord. He has prayed to Him. In essence, he declared, "God has responded to my prayer, and part of my promise to Him is a pledge that I am going to live my life to please Him. Nothing low, nothing vulgar, nothing profane, nothing immoral, nothing dishonest, nothing selfish, nothing unworthy of His presence will reside in my life." This speaks of one's pledge to live before God and mankind in order to honor the Almighty.

Then he speaks of his *persuasion* in verses 10-11. "I believed, therefore have I spoken: I was greatly afflicted: I said in my haste, All men are liars." Now that seems an awfully harsh judgment.

What did he mean by that? I do not think he was making a blanket indictment of all mankind, since there are a few people of commitment and integrity. Some translations render this: "All men are utterly unreliable." He believed; he trusted the Lord. He meant, "The answer is not found in mankind. Humans have no answer to my need." If you want help when you are helpless, you must understand that there is only one person who is totally reliable—and He is God.

Then in verses 12-14 there is *the pattern of his promise.* "What shall I render unto the Lord for all his benefits toward me? I will take the cup of salvation, [I will accept God's offer of salvation] and call upon the name of the Lord. I will pay my vows unto the Lord now in the presence of all his people." He sets before us the pattern of his life: first, he was going to receive what God had given him, and, second, he was going to pay his vows.

In this matter of vows let me remind you that never in the Old Testament were we commanded to give vows to God. God never said we have to promise Him this or that. Rather, what is unfolded in the Old Testament is that, while God does not require vows, if and when we make a vow, we had better keep it! God does not declare we must make a vow. God will judge us severely if we do not keep the vows we have made. I have found out that when God is so good to us, we almost automatically want to make commitments and vows. "I will call upon the name of the Lord" is extremely interesting. Verse 13 speaks not only of fervent communion with God, but that word "call" can also be translated "proclaim." In this sense, to call was a concomitant to "proclaim" —to preach the Word. He would acknowledge publicly that God was and is the Giver of gifts and blessings in his life and ours. He would be a living witness; this would be a continuing pattern of his life. What a promise! "I will walk before the Lord in the land of the living." His promise was committed consistency.

Then he ended this psalm with a heartwarming doxology of *praise,* a climax of gratitude. Here is fervent, passionate thanksgiving to God. He praises God because of the provision He makes. How beautiful is verse 15! "Precious in the sight of the Lord is the death of his saints." Would you believe there are people who have been concerned about what this may mean? All this means is: from God's perspective, the death of His children is a precious event.

Death does not tarnish the glow of the child of God; death does not rob the child of God of victory. Rather, it bestows victory. Paul cried out, "O death, where is thy sting? O grave, where is thy victory? . . . But thanks be to God which giveth the victory through our Lord Jesus Christ" (1 Cor. 15:55-57). Precious, to be valued, to be treasured is the death of God's saints. From God's standpoint death takes the saint from a life of sickness, servitude, and struggle, and transports him into a life of relief, release, and rejoicing. What death becomes to the true child of God, who has put his trust in Christ, is a doorway through which he enters into the eternal presence of God. It is precious for God when we enter perfectly and wholly into His presence at death. Precious!

Then he talks about what God had done in his life. "O Lord, truly I am thy servant; and the son of thine handmaid. Thou hast loosed my bonds" (v. 16). He declared his freedom but at the same time his servitude—"thy servant, and the son of thine handmaid: thou hast loosed my bonds." He was confessing, "God, you have broken the bonds of my sin, but now bind me with the cords of love. Lord, you have freed me from the tyranny of Satan. Now make me as one of your hired servants."

The Old Testament concept of servanthood held that a slave could be set free, and then, if he chose voluntarily to become the servant of his master again, there was a special ceremony by which he voluntarily re-entered servanthood. "You are my liberty," testified the psalmist. "You are my all in all. I lay my life at your feet." Since God had freed him, he would give back his life. I hope you understand that our liberty in Christ is not a license for us to do as we please—but a genuine liberty for us to do as He pleases. It is not a freedom which relieves us of responsibility; it is a freedom which causes us to accept His responsibility. While we are freed from sin and domination of people, we commit ourselves to God. He was freed from the bonds of sin, no longer under its tyranny. We ultimately praise God for His redemption by presenting ourselves back to Him. Paul made that clear when he challenged, "I beseech you therefore, brethren, by the mercies of God, that ye present your bodies a living sacrifice, holy, acceptable unto God, which is your reasonable service" (Rom. 12:1).

Because of what God has done in freeing you from sin, now give Him your body. Give Him your life. There is an element of *praise* for our lives. Then there was:

III. The Profession of the Psalmist

His praise was not only demonstrated by what God had done for him and how he responded to it, but by his own *personal profession.* Verses 17-18: "I will offer to thee the sacrifice of thanksgiving, and will call upon the name of the Lord. I will pay my vows unto the Lord now in the presence of all his people. In the courts of the Lord's house, in the midst of thee, O Jerusalem. Praise ye the Lord." Back in verse 14 he said the same thing—"in the presence of all his people." "Praise ye the Lord" is actually one word—*hallelujah.* He was going to spend the rest of his life in praise and thanksgiving.

Think of the truths in this psalm. He has written, "I love the Lord." "I trust in the Lord." "I will take the salvation of the Lord." "I will pay my vows." "I will walk before the Lord." "I will pray." "I will praise Him." All of those acts of praise were conduits through which he was cultivating the spirit of gratitude. No wonder he drew to a close with that wonderful word *hallelujah.* Praise the Lord. Hallelujah is the same in every language.

What we have observed in this psalm is intensely personal. It is the intimate pilgrimage of the psalmist as he thought about what God had done. The writer related his spiritual autobiography. "I love the Lord," he declared, and all of that is inherent in this psalm. Though this is intimately personal, it is not private, for his love and praise to the Father were not in competition and not excluded from public, formal expressions of commitment. He plainly spoke about paying his vows *in the presence of all the people.* He talked about the courts of the Lord's house and being in the midst of the city of Jerusalem.

Let me suggest that the flame burning in his heart was not withdrawn to burn alone, but rather it was placed in the midst of the congregation where it would kindle others, where it would bless others all the longer and all the better because of it. Here was his public profession and open commitment. What you do with and toward God is very personal. No one can be a proxy for you. That intimate relationship of yours with the Father is a sacred haven no person or group can snatch from you.

But we also have a responsibility to one another to praise the Lord, to live for Him, to commit our lives to Him *together*. We need one another. How many times are we discouraged? We are down and seemingly defeated. Maybe we are ready to "throw in the towel." But another person touches our lives through a song, a lesson, a sermon, a prayer, or through a contact—there is a strange rekindling in our hearts, and the fire begins to burn again!

We depend on one another. We need public worship. We need to live before the Lord in the land of the living. We need to pay our vows unto the Lord in the presence of all His people. We need to come into the courts of the Lord's house, in the midst of the people, to praise Him. Love the Lord. Cultivate the spirit of gratitude in your heart!

11
In Search of Integrity

Psalm 120

Our nation, "the land of the free and the home of the brave," is in a number of urgent crises. The majority of people have not the foggiest notion of what to believe. People say one thing and do another. They say they didn't, but they did. They say they did, but they didn't. We're struggling with a tremendous amount of suspicion and distrust in our nation. The psalmist identified with that national declension. He moaned, "In my distress I cried unto the Lord, and he heard me. Deliver my soul, O Lord, from lying lips, and from a deceitful tongue" (vv. 1-2). We can identify with that. That pungently speaks to our national plight right now.

There was the Iran-Contra affair. Someone was not telling the truth. States and federal governments have gone through more scandals than the tabloids could conjure up. Our eyes and ears were assaulted with the Senate hearing of the confirmation of Judge Clarence Thomas. Every day there is enough governmental mismanagement and corruption to make one disillusioned. Deceit and lies have become common in American society. We were rocked to our economic foundations with the Boeski scandal on Wall Street with his conviction for "insider trading," and several others since then have been convicted of using information gained on the inside of the stock market to make tremendous profits.

Corporate America is finally writing codes of ethics for its employees, trying to keep them honest. Probably 25 percent of the so-called profits in goods you and I buy are tacked on because of employee and customer dishonesty. Stores must add a certain percentage merely to cover the theft that occurs from their employees and their customers. Not long ago there was an investigative study released accusing forty-seven scientists at Harvard Univer-

sity and Emory University Medical Schools of producing mislead-
ing papers. A U.S. House subcommittee recently reported, as best
as it can ascertain, that one out of every three Americans employed
today is working on the basis of falsified credentials. In other
words, they lied about their backgrounds in order to land a
position.

It is a tragedy to the nth degree: Americans are accepting dishonesty as a valid approach to life. No doubt you remember the
foreign car commercial with the lying con man. "Hello," he would
smirk, "I can sell you a new _____ for $9." On the screen ap-
peared, "He's lying. You know, you either get a $500 rebate or a
truck full of bananas." "Not true" was flashed on the screen. Those
ads took the ad world by storm because, down deep inside, most
of us are aware we're being lied to anyway. Here's how it sort of
comes out. Here's the prevalent philosophy. "If I know I'm lying,
and you know I know I'm lying, and I know you know I know I'm
lying, and you know I know you know I'm lying, it's OK." Many
merely accept it. It hits all of us.

Here is the one that slaps the preacher. How many times have
you heard a person ask, "How many did you have at church?"
"Well, we had umpteen folks." Have you heard that? Sometimes
preachers can exaggerate a little bit. Perhaps that is true. Exaggeration is a lie. How many of you employees called in "sick" to do
whatever you wanted, but you were not sick? Is that truthful or
deceitful? You may reply, "You are getting a little too close to
home." Let's come even closer. How many of you have lied about
your income tax deductions? Some reply, "It's OK if you don't get
caught."

You see, American culture differs from most other cultures.
Communist culture, Muslim culture, and most of the other cultures
in the world are based on a system that encourages deceit. We
don't. Free society in American cannot exist apart from integrity.
And Americans expect it. We are discovering that the vast majority
of Americans demand integrity from their public officials, from
their leaders. Strange, we want people we can believe in and trust,
but many have a double standard. If it's wrong for a congressman
to overdraw his back account, it is also wrong for us.

Yet, a lack of integrity is enmeshed with our lives. In New York

City (it was reported in a national magazine) a high-school girl found a purse with $1,000 cash in it, and she returned it! Not one of her school officials would congratulate her for her honesty and virtue. They alibied, "Well, we don't want to begin doing that because that would establish absolutes, and we don't think we ought to do that." That's a bunch of rot!

We'd better wise up. We're raising a group of young people who've never seen integrity, and they will grow up without integrity—lying about their school work, cheating on tests, deceiving their parents. Most kids who are trying to misbehave lie to their parents and teachers about it. But then parents lie to their children, too. Parents often say, "We'll do this if you'll do that," and they don't. Lying has become acceptable. Deceit is approved in our society, and it is a disaster.

We must hear what God says through David: "I said in my haste, All men are liars." Every time I read that I want to shout, "David, say it again, *slowly. 'All men are liars.'* " It is inbred for us to be deceitful. Jesus stated in John 8:44: "Your father, the devil, is a liar. He is a murderer; he is a liar from the beginning" (author's words). There is no truth in Satan, and when we lie we are doing the devil's work. In Job 27:4-5, Job affirmed, "My lips shall not speak wickedness nor my tongue utter deceit. God forbid that I should justify you: till I die I will not remove my integrity from me."

George Gallup, in 1984-85 did a survey of religion in America. It was produced in a book of about 100 pages or so. Certain facts were startling to me. He concluded that crime and immorality—the crime rate—was up in America, but so was religious activity! Then he made a horrific observation: the levels of lying, cheating, and stealing are virtually the same among churchgoers and non-churchgoers. That's an incredible indictment against the church.

Seventy-nine times in the Gospels, Jesus started a statement with, "I tell you the truth." Truthfulness is a mark of godliness, and deceit and lying are a mark of Satan's influence in our lives. In Mark 7:22 deceit is listed among the vices that defile all of life. There ought to be something different about those who claim Jesus Christ as Lord and Savior. Paul in 2 Corinthians 4:2 wrote—we ". . . have renounced the hidden things of dishonesty, not walking in craftiness, nor handling the word of God deceitfully"—manipulating the Word of God to reach our conclusions—"but by manifestation of the truth commending ourselves to every man's conscience in the sight of God."

The psalmist testified, "In my distress I cried unto the Lord, and he heard me. Deliver me O Lord, from lying lips, and from a deceitful tongue." When trust and confidence are broken down in a free society, there are three attitudes that develop. One is *cynicism*. Two is *apathy*, and finally *anarchy*. We in America have already proceeded through the first two. We have become cynical and apathetic, and the next step is sheer anarchy, which is almost the case in Eastern Europe as I write these words, if we do not rediscover our roots in integrity.

Now this Psalm speaks to four aspects of integrity. First of all, it refers to:

I. The Psalmist's Distress

"In my distress I cried unto the Lord, and he heard me" (v. 1). First of all, the psalmist speaks about the *agony* of it. "In my distress"—the very word "distress" connotes an agonizing, torturous experience in our lives. He apparently was remembering times in the past when he was lied about, when he was slandered. Who of us would not admit it is painful to be lied about? When there have been deceit and slander against us, it has hurt ferociously. It distresses one's spirit, but I think this means more than that. I believe the liar also endures agony. The one who slanders, lies in a perpetual hell—agony. There is nothing good in falsehood. Oh, the agony and distress of dishonesty!

Then he touched on the answer. "In my distress I cried unto the Lord . . ." and that's the best thing to do. Cry out to God. Many times it's useless to appeal to your friends because, when you do, you may spread the problem even more. And it's certainly useless appealing to your slanderers because they have no honor in the first place, or they wouldn't have slandered you. If you do appeal to them, all you do is sharpen their determination to increase their malignity and spur them on to new accusations. No, when you are slandered, when you are lied about, you have only one recourse, and that is God. I would quickly emphasize that whatever drives us to God is ultimately good. It is futile appealing to friends or those who attack us. Turn to God. Where our weakness lies, there is God's strength, and He is there.

Here is the distress of falsehood, the sheer acuteness of it. The answer: call unto the Lord. Then he speaks of:

II. The Psalmist's Deliverance

"Deliver me," he literally prays. "Deliver my soul, O Lord, from lying lips, and from a deceitful tongue" (v. 2). From the very beginning of God's Word, it tells us we ought to be truthful. As far back as Exodus 20:16, in the Ten Commandments, it teaches that we must not bear false witness. Do not lie about your neighbor. Do not slander him or her. In Leviticus 19:11,16, God said, "Ye shall not steal, neither deal falsely, neither lie one to another." You shall not go up and down as a talebearer among your people. That's written into the basic relationship we have with God, so the psalmist cries for deliverance against those who violate those commands.

He speaks first about falsehood. "Deliver my soul, O Lord, from lying lips." From lying lips. Only the person who has experienced the pain and harm springing from lies will understand that what the psalmist is talking about is not a light matter, not casual but deadly serious. Falsehood. Lying is a malignant cancer that destroys all it touches, an insidious evil that corrupts from the inside out.

There are several ways people can lie. One is by rumors. Rumors are lies born in hell. They corrupt those who begin them and those who pass them on. For instance, have you recently heard someone remark, "They did this. They did that?" Most of the time what you are hearing is a lie. Who are *they?* What are their names? What did they do? Did you see it? Can you verify it yourself? Is it absolutely certain that such and such occurred?

Now we Christians have a more sophisticated manner of doing it. "We need to pray for so and so. They're having these terrible problems, and"—what is really a need to pray for them becomes a vehicle of telling this or that which hurts them. Simply because something is true doesn't give you a right to spread it. I know certain facts about many that do not need to be broadcast. I have heard in my office and in my contacts day by day innuendos that do not need to be repeated. They are often true, but I would be wrong to repeat them.

We must be careful how we hide deceit and slander behind the guise of "praying" for a person. Such is deceitful in itself. Sometimes rumors are true, but they can be used deceitfully. Sometimes we mix truth and rumors, and we use them because we realize it will hurt a person or persons. Who of us has not been affected by such? I myself have been hurt deeply in the last few years because lies and half-truths were spread with deliberate intent to hurt me. Some may have been true—in a sense. Let me give you an example.

Calvin Miller, now a professor at Southwestern Seminary, confesses that one time when he was a seminary student he had to study for a test. He knew he had to study all day—he was working nights—if he were going to pass the test, but he also had to go to work. He didn't want to tell his boss that he needed to study, so he hit upon an ingenious plan. He and his wife were going to have fish sticks for supper so he lay on the bed and asked her to give him the frozen fish sticks. He pitched them up into the air and caught them. And he said, "Now you call my boss and tell him that I'm 'flat on my back' and just threw up my dinner."

Now, let me ask you: Was that true? Yes. Sure, it was true. Was it honest? No. Was it deceitful? Yes. It was deliberately designed to deceive. Now we can identify with that because we've all been there more than likely.

I know one businessman in Galveston, Texas, who had over his office door the name "Houston." And when he didn't want to talk with someone, his secretary would report—"He's not here. He's in Houston." Was that true? In one sense, sure. He was in—that's what it said—"Houston." That was dishonest. You can see how suddenly this subterfuge worms its way into our lives until nothing is sacred. If people can get away with it, standards of honesty are violated.

There is one truth we seem not to understand about Scripture. Scripture is based on the principle of a covenant. All we do is to be based on the principle of a covenant. There's a difference between a covenant and a contract. With a contract, people look for ways to break it. With a covenant, you cannot break a covenant.

That is why one day God is going to send His Son, and Jesus Christ will rule and reign through all of eternity, and He will reveal Himself again to those living Jews at that time, and they will respond to the gospel. Why? Because God has a covenant with Israel, and He is going to keep His covenant.

There are so many divorces because men and women look upon their marriage as a contract. No, it is not a contract. It is a covenant. If one understands it as a covenant, it will not be quite so easy to break. If it's a contract one will look for an escape clause. Many have learned to use the truth deceitfully, and it is tragic when that happens to us.

John White in his book called *The Race* writes of a young man who told a malicious story about an older man in the community. Then he became convicted about it and apologized to the man. He asked, "What can I do to make it right?" The old man had the young acquaintance bring his pillow. The elderly fellow went up into the belfry of the church, had the fellow tear open the pillowcase, and then flap that case over the side. The feathers blew to the four winds until they scattered all over the countryside. Then the old man said, "Now go pick them up."

The young man protested, "Well, that's impossible. I can't pick them up." And he was right. But that's exactly what happens when you slander or lie about a person.

Have you ever noticed that accusations are on page 1 in the paper and retractions are on page 27 in the "E" section? You can't do it. The blatant tragedy of slander and deceit is that we do not realize how terrible they are. All I have in this world is my reputation. Do not steal it from me. Do not pluck it away from me. Do not accuse me, slander me.

Shakespeare observed: "He who takes my riches, steals trash from me, but he who steals my good name takes that which not enriches him and makes me poor indeed." Deceit. Slander. "O God, deliver me from lying lips." In Ephesians 4:25 and 29, Paul admonished,

> Wherefore putting away lying, speak every man truth with his neighbor: for we are members one of another . . . Let no corrupt communication proceed out of your mouth, but that which is good to the use of edifying, that it may minister grace unto the hearers.

Paul pled in Colossians 3:9 and 10, Don't lie one to another, "seeing that ye have put off the old man with his deeds; And have put on the new man, which is renewed in knowledge after the image of him that created him." Put it away. God, deliver me from lying lips.

The point of telling the truth is love—love of integrity, love of trust, love for other people. But when truth is told maliciously, only honesty is served. When truth is told in kindness, then both honesty and love are served. Love is to be truthful to people in such a fashion that they learn to trust us because truth breeds trust. Lies breed distrust. That's why Jesus said, "Let your yea be yea, and your nay be nay." Be transparent. Be true.

The psalmist wrote that there needed to be *deliverance from falsehood,* and also *deliverance from flattery* and from a deceitful tongue. Flattery is to take words and use them in trying to gain an advantage. We attempt to flatter a person so they will do what we want them to do. Now I'm a "patsy" for that. I'm a sucker for it. "Man, if you'll do this. You're the only one in the world who can." That sounds good, even great. Flattery. "Flattery will get you anywhere," we comment. You see, that's worse than outright lies because it is taking words and using them to deceive. You'd better meet wild beasts and serpents than a flatterer. A deceiver. They twist and pervert the truth with a smile and a backslap. But watch out. They may have a knife in there somewhere, and you will feel its point.

Psalm 12:2 and 4 observes, "They speak vanity every one with his neighbor: with flattering lips and with a double heart do they speak. The Lord shall cut off all flattering lips, and the tongue that speaks proud things: Who have said, With our tongue will we prevail; our lips are our own: who is lord over us?" And there are people today who have mastered the art of lying and deceiving. There must be a deliverance. You can understand why the psalmist sang, "O God, deliver me from lying lips and a deceitful heart."

Then he spoke of:

III. The Deceiver's Destruction

The point of verses 3 and 4 is: it's serious to lie, to deceive others. So he wrote about the *seriousness* of it and then the *sentence* of it, the conclusion and judgment of it.

First, the *seriousness* of it. Proverbs 10:18 noted, "He who hides hatred with lying lips and he who utters a slander is a fool." That is God speaking. He who deceives, who slanders, who lies is a fool. Proverbs 6:16-19 lists six things "God hates"—"Yea seven are an abomination to God," and four of them relate to lies and deceit. Certainly a proud look and feet that are swift to create mischief are partners in that, or closely related to that. God despises these sins.

Verse 3 of this psalm is a rhetorical question. "What shall be given unto thee or what shall be done unto thee, thou false tongue?" In other words, who will respond to the liar? And the thrust of it is—*God will*. That's how serious it is. God himself is going to answer. In Nahum 3:1, the prophet wailed—"Woe to the bloody city!" That sounds bad, doesn't it? "Woe to the bloody city! It is all full of lies and robbery," which is a form of deceit. A lie. In Hosea 4:1-2, the prophet indicated the Lord had a controversy with the inhabitants of the land because there was no truth there. By swearing, by lying, by killing, by stealing, and by committing and permitting adultery, they break out, and blood touches blood. In Psalm 120:3 the psalmist in effect was saying, "Do you understand what happens to people who engage in such malicious deceit? Do you know what happens to people who lie and deceive?" God Himself is going to intervene.

What will God do with liars? We are certain of this. He has uttered His most terrible threats against them, and He will execute judgment on them in due time. Why is truth so vital? Because God is a God of truth. That's why. God requires truth. Lying is an abomination to Him, according to Proverbs 12, and Proverbs 6 declares He hates lying. So here is the seriousness of deceit, slander, and lies.

Now what is the *sentence* of it? Verse 4 tells us what the psalmist would do. What kind of a judgment is the liar going to face? Verse 4 is a form of judgment that the psalmist himself has thought up, but the bottom line is that the liar, though he has sharp weapons with his tongue and though he uses his words to wound many, will be destroyed with far more potent shafts than his lies—God's arrows of truth, God's coals of judgment. You can be sure that the sentence will be carried out.

Psalm 101:5-7:

Whoever privily slanders his neighbor, him will I cut off. Him that hath a high look and a proud heart will not I suffer. I will not tolerate him.My eyes shall be upon the faithful of the land that they may dwell with me: he who walks in a perfect way shall serve me, but he who works deceit shall not dwell within my house and he who tells lies shall not tarry, shall not stand in my sight.

That's the sentence of it. God himself will enter in.

The last three verses (5-7) speak of dissension. For anywhere there are lies, distortion, deceit, and slander, there are dissension and strife. Write it down. Anywhere that goes on, you will have a mess. And that's what he describes in these three verses. This is a classic statement about the incompatibility of light and darkness. They cannot go together. Lies are not of God, and they can never be compatible with truthfulness. Deceit is an ungodly characteristic. It can never mesh with integrity. There is always a conflict between evil and good, a clash between light and darkness. These verses describe that.

He describes disharmony in verses 5 and 6. He did not live in the midst of those people he was describing here, but the people he did live with had the same characteristics. Notice he wrote: "Woe is me, that I sojourn in Mesech, that I dwell in the tents of Kedar." That was almost like saying, "from the Atlantic to the Pacific."

Mesech was a tribe on the southeast of the Black Sea. It was a long distance from Israel. Kedar was a tribe in the desert of Syria, south of Damascus. They were far removed from each other and from Israel. We are aware from history that Mesech and Kedar were barbarous, violent tribes. What the psalmist meant figuratively was that liars among whom he lived were utterly uncivilized and cruel. One of the cruelest persons in the world is a liar, a deceiver, a slanderer. It is not pleasant to live with them. The psalmist moaned, "I can endure it no more." My soul hath long dwelt with him that hateth peace: (v. 6). He was out of patience. He could handle it no more. There was *discord*, dissension.

Then he wrote of:

IV. The Psalmist's Disposition

It was a mild complaint. He was not being boastful. He argued, "I'm not the one who created this problem. I'm not the one who initiated this situation. I am for peace, but my opposition is for war. There is unreasonable hostility, and what results is bitter strife and contention." I wish we could somehow understand the severity of this psalm. There is no human method of dealing with a liar. Only God can do that. If only we would all understand what we do when we lie, when we deceive! Do you perceive that most criticism expressed in a church is deceitful? For you'll hear people ask, "Did you hear what the staff did?" When did they do it? That's deceitful. It's deliberately spreading distrust.

Let me ask you a question. Why would you spread a criticism that is nothing more than a rumor and slander against people you love? Can you answer that? Why would you do that? *They* say. Who are *they?* This kind of spirit and this untoward use of the tongue creates nothing but dissension and disharmony. Listen, if they are as bad as you claim they are, go somewhere else. Get out. You do not help by deceiving and slandering people. You may say—"Well, I just tell the truth." No, you don't. You tell *part* of the truth.

Let me give you an illustration. We had in and out of our church office a flood of people. I used to see an average of ten people a day. That was over 3,500 a year. All of our staff members were as busy as I was. It may be that at the church one day a person came in and requested, "I want to see the pastor." And the word came back, "The pastor can't see you now." And maybe that person or some-one else commented, "Somebody came to see the pastor, really needed the pastor, and the pastor wouldn't see him!"

And they began to tell others—"Did you hear what the pastor did?" What that person may not have known was that I had been with that man until 4 o'clock in the morning. I had spent hours and hours with him. There is a limit to one's amount of time. You see, one person saw part of the truth. What was repeated was slander-ous. "Well, I saw." You don't know what you saw. You don't know the circumstances of it.

I graded papers for Dr. Kyle Yates in Baylor University when I was a student. He was one of the kindest men I've ever known. I asked him one day why he was so kind. I said, "You're the most tender, kind-hearted man I've ever known."

He replied, "Well, when I was a seminary professor, there was a young man who came into my 8 o'clock class in the morning and slept through every class. I watched him sleep and just became more and more infuriated until finally I said to the fellow: 'Young man, you wake up and stand up in front of me.' He stood up and I blessed him out."

"I told him he shouldn't come back to that class until he could stay awake, until he could be better prepared. After the class was over someone came up to me and said—'Dr. Yates, I wish you hadn't done that.' I asked 'why?' He answered, 'because that young man's wife is in the hospital dying of cancer. He spends most of his hours with her when he can. He works full-time all night and comes to school in addition to that. I wish you hadn't done that, Dr. Yates.'"

He said, "I felt so small. I didn't know. All I knew was what I saw. I vowed I'd never be unkind to anybody again."

When you see something you don't know why it was done. When you hear something you don't know why it was said. And when you repeat it in a way to cause harm and to create a certain kind of impression, you are a liar, a deceiver, and a slanderer, and God will judge you. That's strong language, isn't it? But it's the truth.

Deliver me from lying lips and a deceitful tongue, making promises I don't keep—using people through flattery and deception. It's common in our society. We have to stop and consciously commit ourselves to the Lord not to do it. Exaggeration, "white" lies, "little" untruths—we've come to accept them. But 1 Peter 3:10 says, "He that will love life, and see good days, let him refrain his tongue from evil, and his lips that they speak no guile."

Do you want to enjoy life while you are alive? Do you want to extend your life? Then refrain your lips from evil and from deceit and from lying. Do you want to know what God's attitude is? Read Acts 5 again about Ananias and Sapphira when they came and made their offering to God. They didn't claim that was all of their gift. Everybody else was giving *all* of their possessions. They came and gave their possessions. They didn't lie with their lips; they just left the wrong impression. They merely *appeared* to be giving everything. Everybody thought they had, and that couple didn't correct the impression. Peter said, "You've lied to the Holy Spirit," and they carried them out dead. That's how much God hates deception. Lying.

None of us are exempt from it. You remember when I point a finger at you that three others are pointing back at me. We've grown up in this kind of culture, and we need to understand that God hates lies. God abhores deceit. Now we must endeavor to be honest people. Remember Paul's words in Philippians 4:8, "Finally, brethren, whatsoever things are true, whatsoever things are honest, whatsoever things are just, whatsoever things are pure, whatsoever things are lovely, whatsoever things are of good report; if there be any virtue, and if there be any praise, think on these things." But then he went on to say, "Those things, which ye have both learned, and received, and heard, and seen in me, do: and the God of peace shall be with you" (v. 9).

Do you want God's presence in your life? Do the truth. Live the truth. Truth is not just something you believe; it is something you do. So be a *doer* of truth. Keep your lips from lies, from deceit. It brings agony and distress to the people who receive the slander and those who dish it out. It is a distressing situation.

But the psalmist wrote, "In my distress I cried unto the Lord . . ." and I suggest to you—whatever drives you to God is good. So you've been the victim? Go to God with it. So you found yourself using those tactics yourself? Go to God with it. God will bless you for it.

12
Strength for Tough Times

Psalm 138

Why are the Psalms relevant 3,000 years after they were composed by David and other musicians under the inspiration of the Holy Spirit? Because we discover ourselves on "the sacred page" —we think and feel with the psalmists . . . their sadness and gladness, their fellowship with God but also their emotions of estrangement, their victories and defeats, the entire gamut of ups and downs.

David was to be the forerunner of the Messiah Himself. He had been promised that when the Messiah came, He would sit upon David's throne. In spite of God's never-failing promises, kingdom matters were messed up when this was written. It bolsters me to realize that David, so secure in the promises of God, could have hard times, even as we do. What did he do when hard times came? What was his recourse when circumstances collapsed around him and seemed to threaten his very existence?

God has a special word for people having hard times. Do you ever undergo hard times? I surely do. This comforting psalm falls into three logical divisions. The first three verses I call *worship*; the next three, *wonder*; and the last two, the *walk* of the man amid trouble. What does he do as he walks through trouble?

First, there is:

I. Worship for Hard Times

Verses 1-3 reveal the outpouring of a grateful heart for many recent blessings of God in his life. First he expresses the bountiful praise of his heart:

I will praise thee with my whole heart: before the gods will I sing praise unto thee. I will worship toward thy holy temple, and praise thy name for thy lovingkindness and for thy truth: for thou hast magnified thy word above all thy name. In the day when I cried thou answeredst me, and strengthenedst me with strength in my soul.

Verse 1 and 2 reveal the *expression* of *worship*, and verse 3 shows the *extremity out of which he worshiped*.

In these first two verses he resolves to praise God for all that He has done. I like that phrase: "I will praise thee with my whole heart." Really, how can you praise God any other way? How can you praise God half-heartedly? Many people serve God like they're half asleep, like there is nothing to be excited about, nothing to be rejoicing over, nothing to be grateful for.

For the psalmist it was "all or nothing at all." To use common slang, "Just turn everything loose, and give it the very best shot you possibly can." Even though David, being a devout Jew, might not have approved—down South if you do something really big, you do it "whole hog." However you phrase it, that's how I want to praise God and serve Him. If you're going to do it, for the sake of the Lord, do it. "Give of your best to the master."

He was not going to be restrained because people around him didn't appreciate it. Notice the phrase: "Before the gods will I sing praise unto thee"—in other words, before all of those who claimed authority, those who tried to be gods in people's lives, before the false gods of the world, all the untruths of other religions and heresies. He was going to praise the Lord in spite of what people thought. In the middle of God's enemies, he was going to sing praises unto God. Years ago there was a book entitled *Praise the Lord—Anyhow*. The truth is: if other folks won't praise God that's all the more reason why we should.

Out there in the marketplace you hear men and women taking the name of God in vain. There used to be public laws against that, in addition to a violation of the Ten Commandments. I submit to you, if they can take God's name in vain, we ought to be able to praise God. Praise Him publicly and privately. It doesn't matter whether or not they approve, but let the praises of God course from your hearts. Stand for God. Do they deny the Deity of the Lord? Then let us love Him as Deity Incarnate. Do they deny the atoning grace of God? Then let us proclaim it and teach it with all of the energy of our beings. When folks oppose God, let us stand for Him.

Let us sing praises to God. Singing and praising are the weapons of our warfare as we defend the gospel and as we face opposition from those around us. As we receive comfort for depression that often settles in upon us because of our circumstances, songs and praises will prevail. One writer exclaimed that the hallelujah legion is going to win out. I believe that as we praise God.

David had seen the mercy of God in his life and in the lives of others. He was conscious of God confirming His Word and keeping His promises. In light of that the psalmist wanted to become a herald for God. He wanted to shout it out loud. God had fulfilled His promise dramatically and it gave David a glimpse of God that he had not seen before. His heart was amazed by the magnitude of that recent blessing. That was all he could think about. "Thou hast magnified thy word above all thy name" (v. 1b).

There is an excellent lesson here. On the surface this statement sounds incorrect. Perhaps he does not seem to be employing theologically correct terms because we are aware that no single act of God can ever surpass His name. In fact, every act of God enhances and further reveals the name and character of God, because the name of God refers to His very being. No single act of God is greater than God Himself. So, if you want to use narrowly defined theological terms, then, technically speaking, that is an incorrect statement.

But you must read between the lines, as it were. David had just discovered a marvelous new moving of God in his life. God had confirmed the truthfulness and faithfulness of His Word, and He had done what He promised he would do. The psalmist was absolutely overwhelmed with the greatness of God. He was not preaching, not teaching, but singing a song of thanksgiving. He felt that the most current moving of God in his life was the sweetest experience he had ever known.

It ought to be like that with us. We sometimes have sung the little chorus, "Everyday with Jesus Is Sweeter than the Day Before." Actually, He Himself is not sweeter today than He was yesterday. The day is sweeter. We simply learn a little more about Him today. Jesus can't change. He is infinite perfection of sweetness, of purity, and of holiness. He is all of those—and more. David has had an expanded encounter with God, which enhanced and enlarged his vision of God. It deepened his appreciation of God, and so he burst forth in thanksgiving and praise to the Almighty. God does not mind that at all. I don't think God minds when we say, "Lord, You are more marvelous today than you were yesterday." God could dispute with us about it, "No, I was fully as marvelous yesterday as I am today. I am the same. I change not." No. God is pleased when, with overflowing gratitude, we thank Him for who He is and what He has done. We are to praise Him out of a grateful heart and a thankful spirit.

When God confirms His Word and when He keeps His promise to us, then the whole being of God assumes a new luster, a new excitement, and a new blessing for us. So David expressed his worship with reckless abandon, praising God before all the authorities and even the enemies and opponents of God. He praised God, and he exuberantly declared "What You have done is the most marvelous experience I have ever enjoyed. Note:

II. The Psalmist's Extremity

"In the day when I cried you answered me, and strengthened me with strength in my soul" (v. 3). There are several important facts in this verse. The first is: this verse shows us *the distinguishing mark* of the true and living God. What sets God apart from every other so-called god in the world? The living memorial for the true God is—He hears the prayers of His people. The gods of wood and stone, the idols, the temples of spiritism, and the pagan religions of the world—those gods have no ears to hear and no hand to move, but our God hears the cries of His people. He is a God who responds to our needs.

David cried. Amid ecstasy he was also burdened with more agony than usual. He cried because he was weak, because he was wounded, because he was worried, because he was weary. He cried, and God answered. It is exciting that the word "cried" is the same you would use for a baby crying. He could not even articulate; he simply knew he was hurting. He was having hard times. So he cried to God and God heard and God answered.

That is a majestic truth about God. If you reach out to Him, He understands what you want. If you reach out for God (even if you don't have the words to express yourself), God will answer. People often come to me and mention, "Preacher, I just don't know whether I said the right words when I asked Jesus to come into my heart, or when I prayed I don't know if I said the right words."

I have electrifying news for you. It's not your words He's interested in. It's the cry of your heart. When your heart cries out to Him, when you hurt, when your pain is real, and you simply direct that toward God, He hears and answers and interprets your pain. He understands our cries, and He responds to our needs. Cry to God. Weep to God. Lift your hurt and your wounded spirit to God. Reach to Him, and He is ever-present.

But this verse also relates *how He answers*. Notice. The psalmist noted that You "strengthenedst me with strength in my soul." That is not really what most of us want to hear. We would like to read, You strengthened me by "zapping" my enemies. To us that would be better. "You strengthened me by changing my circumstances." "You strengthened me by restoring my position." "You strengthened me by breaching the gap that has come in my relationship." But those thoughts were not even expressed. He literally sang, "You strengthened me with strength in my heart and soul." He was saying that if the burden was not removed, He still gives you strength enough to bear it. God is not interested in merely removing our difficulties. If He were, we wouldn't need Him. God is concerned with being Himself in us, and thus affording us strength to meet the difficulties we face. That is how God does it most of the time.

Now there are periods when God may alter circumstances, may heal broken relationships, may change the situation we find ourselves in—but the truth is, what we need is not different circumstances; we need to be different people. In most instances it is not the situation that must be changed—it is the individual that must be changed. We don't like to hear that because we have the idea that if we could only make a change, it would solve our problems.

That's why many people divorce and marry. That's why many people change jobs; why many people move from one community to another. They do it because they think if they could only change their circumstances. . . . The truth is: if we ourselves don't change, then we have the same old person in new circumstances, and we will create the same kind of problems we had before. "I cried to You. I was desperate," prayed David. The wall had collapsed. "I was having hard times. I cried to You, and You heard me and answered me, and here's how you answered me—You gave me strength in my soul."

Isn't that Paul's message in 1 Corinthians 12 when he wrote about "a thorn in the flesh, a messenger of Satan to buffet me"? Satan had targeted him, had singled him out, had afflicted him. And he asked God to remove that affliction. And God said, "My grace is sufficient for thee." So Paul understood and said, "Therefore I'll glory in my infirmity and my weakness, for when I'm weak, then I'm strong."

When God changes us and strengthens us in our inner being we are able to deal with the circumstances of life. Every hard time we have to face is but an opportunity for us to enter into the strength of God in our hearts. It is an opportunity for us to walk in a new dimension of spirituality with the Lord. He cried. God heard. God answered. God strengthened him in his heart. God gave him the grace to bear what he faced.

You remark, "Preacher, I don't know about that. I'm having hard times. I sure would like things to change." I understand that. There have been many times in my life when I wished I could change what had happened, when I wished I could alter the circumstances I found myself in. You can surely identify with this. When you discover yourself in circumstances you want to change, the greatest temptation and tendency you have is to become angry, bitter at God and at people, mad at whoever is involved. How we long for change. Frankly, most of the time God is not going to change the circumstances. You come back with, "Well, how then can I have victory?" It's so simple—on your knees before God.

"God, I'm hurting. My world has collapsed. I'm having hard times. I'm facing things I can't stand. God, I wish and pray. Lord, I pray somehow these circumstances could be changed, but, God, I'm going to trust in You, I'm going to love You, I'm going to serve You. If the circumstances never change, if the situation is never any different, if the relationship is never healed, I'm going to love You just the same. I'm going to serve You until I die." When you can make that your prayer, strange things are going to happen to and in you. You're going to find strength in your soul. Anger, hostility, bitterness, resentment, resistance—all of these are energies of the flesh that are doomed to fail. The only means of finding light in the dark tunnel of hard times is to discover for ourselves the strength of the Lord in our lives. He was in extremity, but he found the strength of the Lord for himself. Well there's *worship*.

Verses 4 to 6 contain what I would call *wonder* because of what God has promised. God had promised an eternal kingdom for David, and as he looked toward the fulfillment of the promise not yet fulfilled (for that kingdom had not and has not been established in an eternal fashion), he had high hopes. The Messiah had not come. He had not established His reign upon the earth. But there is coming a time when the words of God must be declared around the world, when all God promised will be revealed and be fulfilled to the last detail. It will not be forever hidden. Every tongue must confess that He is Lord, and His words must be spread throughout all the earth.

In the wonder of that magnificent truth the psalmist thought of a time when, "All the kings of the earth shall praise thee, O Lord . . ." and "they will sing in the ways of the Lord: for great is the glory of the Lord" (vv. 4-5).

He spoke of the wonder that all of the mighty people of the world are going to praise God. "Oh, the wonder of it all." All of the nations and all of the authoritative, influential people in the world will praise God. But he also wondered not only that the mighty people will praise God, but that God is interested in the meek "lowly" people. Look at verse 6. "Though the Lord is high, yet hath he respect unto the lowly: but the proud he knows afar off." Though God be high, He has interest in, respect for those that are low. This was a dramatic approach to talking about the differences between God and humanity. God is so great that He is interested in the most insignificant person on earth. Amazing!

God does not love you because you're important. You're important because God loves you! There is nothing in you to make God love you. There is nothing in you to require God to love you. In our humanistic society we want to think that there are inherently worthwhile and valuable qualities about every individual, but the truth is—"all have sinned and come short of the glory of God," and "all of our righteousnesses are as filthy rags" in the sight of God.

It is mystifying that this high, holy, and eternal God has regard for folks like you and me. You say, "Oh, my problems are so small." No they're not. Anything that concerns you concerns Him; anything that touches you touches Him. He is a faithful high priest, the writer of Hebrews writes, who is touched with the feeling of our infirmities. When I hurt, He hurts. What hurts me hurts Him. We're in this together. He cares for us. What a wonder that God should care for us like that.

Look at those last two verses:

> Though I walk in the midst of trouble, thou wilt revive me: thou shalt stretch forth thine hand against the wrath of mine enemies, and thy right hand shall save me. The Lord will perfect that which concerns me: thy mercy, O Lord, endures for ever: forsake not the works of thine hands (vv. 7-8).

Well David was still in trouble, walking in the midst of trouble. He was not bogged down in it, not overcome by it, not overwhelmed by it. He was walking in it. The very fact he was walking in it indicated he was going to pass through it. "This, too, shall pass." He was going through it. He did not run or race through it—he walked through it. Though he walked through "the valley of the shadow of death," he did not walk alone. The great God was with him, walking beside him.

Verse 7 demonstrates that God was still in control of the battle. Verse 8 speaks to us of that complete victory that will be ours through Christ Jesus. When we walk through trouble we have good company, for God is near to pour fresh life into us. If we receive reviving, then we need not regret the trouble. I think of the passage in Daniel when the three Hebrew children were thrown into the fiery furnace. They don't avoid the fiery furnace; they were thrown into it. When Nebuchadnezzar peered into that furnace, remember his words. "Lo, I see four men loose walking in the midst of the fire, and they have no hurt, and the form of the fourth is like the Son of God."

That's how it is. When trouble comes we walk through it, but we will never walk alone if the Son of God is with us. We have the Lord with us—His presence, His strength. Without Him it would be unbearable. Without Him what could we do? Without Him how could we stand it? Verse 8 also treats the trust we can have in Him. "The Lord will perfect or will complete that which concerns us." What a tremendous statement that is. Our assurance is firm. What God is doing He will complete in due season.

God is not like the foolish tower builder in Luke 14 who started to build and couldn't finish. God always finishes what He starts. He never stops until He has completed His work. God's Word is perfect. Man's work is clumsy and incomplete, but God does not stop until He has finished. This verse is glorious to me. The Lord will perfect what concerns Him. Here are two touching elements of prayer. Here is confidence expressed and petition asked.

Could I paraphrase it? "Lord, I know you're going to finish everything You started concerning me. Please hurry up and do it." "Lord, I know you are going to finish it. Do it. I know, God, this is Your plan; this is what You've said. You will keep Your Word. You will do what you said. Now, Lord, don't fail to do what you said." Here is a statement of confidence and a petition, a request for God to do it. It is entirely consistent with who God is. That middle phrase in the verse explains it. "For thy mercy, O Lord, endures forever." God is going to do it, so I can express confidence in it, and I can petition Him to move on with it. All of our interests are safe in God's hands. If you give them to Him, God is going to respond.

All of America stood breathless for sixty hours when Jessica McClure, an eighteen-month-old baby, had fallen into a narrow pipe to an abandoned water well in Midland, Texas. It seemed as if the whole country stopped for two and one-half days. People flew in from all over the country to offer assistance and help. Strong men worked incessantly, never leaving the site, trying to free her. How many millions of dollars were spent on freeing a baby girl? She became front-page news, capturing the imagination of the nation. We were in a meeting at our church with some adults when the news of her rescue was announced. Guess what we did. We applauded. We were so caught up in it. We had a part in it. We had prayed for her. Because we prayed for her and were interested in her, we had a part in her deliverance, her freedom. Isn't that amazing?

An eighteen-month-old girl was so significant that the news even reported about an operation on her right foot. When was an operation on the foot of a baby girl in Midland, Texas, front-page news? Why? She had a need. People could hear her cry. She didn't know how to tell her rescuers—"My foot's pinned." She didn't know how to tell them, "My circulation is not proper." She didn't know how to tell them what she needed. She cried, and the whole country stopped and worked and prayed for her to be saved. Grown people did unusual things. In Midland, Texas, when she was pulled out they cheered, and then all across that Midland-Odessa area people drove through town honking their horns, waving, clapping, cheering—for Jessica was saved.

If in America, with all of our problems and all of our difficulties, we could stand breathless for sixty hours and pour all of our energy and all of our intelligence into saving the physical life of a baby, don't you think that Almighty God can meet your need when you cry, can come to meet you at the point of your hurt, your pain?

We are common folks, yet we cared. How much more does God care? How much more does God want to give us strength in the inner soul, strength to meet the challenge, strength to face the disappointment? There is strength for hard times if you will commit your life to Jesus Christ.